Who Are the Children of Lehi?

Who Are the Children of Lehi?

DNA and the Book of Mormon

D. Jeffrey Meldrum and Trent D. Stephens

GREG KOFFORD BOOKS
SALT LAKE CITY, 2007

Published in the USA

2011   5 4 3 2
Greg Kofford Books, Inc.
P.O. Box 1362
Draper, UT 84020
www.koffordbooks.com

Library of Congress Cataloging-in-Publication Data

Meldrum, Jeff.
    Who are the children of Lehi? : DNA and the Book of Mormon / Jeff Meldrum & Trent Stephens.
        p. cm.
    Includes index.
    ISBN 978-1-58958-129-6
    1. Book of Mormon. 2. Lehi (Book of Mormon figure) 3. Indians--Origin. 4. DNA studies. I. Stephens, Trent D. II. Title.
    BX8627.M45 2007
    289.3'22--dc22

2007047310

Contents

Chapter One
The Book of Mormon: Literal or Literary?

"Who are the children of Lehi?" and "How can the story of Lehi and his children, as told in the Book of Mormon, be reconciled with modern DNA data?" are questions of interest and significance to many people, especially Latter-day Saints.[1] Some people maintain the aspiration that DNA research will either vindicate or refute the Book of Mormon as a historical record of America's ancient inhabitants, whether to bolster their own faith, to persuade the nonbeliever, or conversely, to justify their rejection of the document as an ancient historical record.

Our perspective in writing this book is that of faithful Latter-day Saints who view the Book of Mormon as an accurate account of actual historic events. We are also biologists. Jeff is an anthropologist and anatomist. Trent is a developmental biologist and anatomist. Although our primary research interests center on areas other than genetics, our respective backgrounds and training, as well as our teaching responsibilities, include significant components of molecular genetics and population genetics. As scientists, we accept the DNA data published by genetic anthropologists researching Native American origins while recognizing the inherent limitations to sampling the genetics of populations and the challenges of interpreting the raw data. We view those data as clearly and reasonably representing an American-Asian connection for the majority, if not the whole, of the present-day native populations of the New World.

But we also acknowledge that this conclusion does *not* constitute a refutation of the historicity of the Book of Mormon. It is only with a combined understanding of the sometimes-subtle details of the primary Book of Mormon account and the complex nature of inheritance that one can attempt to reconcile the written record of the children of Lehi with the genetic legacy of Native American populations studied to date. We contend that the apparent contradiction stems from imposing simplistic generalizations onto the primary account, placing undue significance on speculations by early Church officials, or failing to recognize the limitations on the interpretation of the genetic legacies of populations.

We became specifically engaged with these questions when we were jointly invited to participate on a panel discussion at the 2001 Sunstone Symposium at Salt Lake City titled "DNA and Lamanite Identity: A Galileo Event?" The moderator and participant, Brent Lee Metcalfe, a technical editor in the computer industry, stated in the symposium abstract, "Genetic research promises to help genealogists define and refine family trees. But this technological blade can cut both ways. What is a benefit to LDS genealogists may be a detriment to Book of Mormon literalists. Initial findings of geneticists have so far failed to link Native American populations to ancient Israelites."[2] Metcalfe and the fourth panelist, Thomas Murphy, an anthropologist at Edmunds Community College in the state of Washington, adopted a position that modern DNA evidence fails to support the assumption that American Indians are somehow genealogically connected to Israelites or Jews and that the historicity of the Book of Mormon is therefore thrown into question.[3]

We agreed at the time and continue to agree today that genetic findings among Native Americans have failed to link Native American populations to ancient Israelites. We pointed out, however, a number of other considerations that must be included when analyzing and interpreting the data. Those considerations and others are the substance of this book. At the conclusion of the panel discussion, a member of the audience asked (to paraphrase), "Archeologists haven't found one bit of evidence to support the

Book of Mormon, and now molecular biology has failed to produce any support. When are you just going to accept that the Book of Mormon is a work of fiction from the nineteenth century?" One is certainly at liberty to adopt such an opinion, but the point we made then—and the point we continue to make now—is that one must be very careful in how scientific data are interpreted. Stating that there are no modern genetic connections between Native American and Middle Eastern populations does not justify a statement that no such connections ever existed or that the Book of Mormon is a work of nineteenth-century fiction.

Numerous examples of sweeping generalizations, oversimplifications, and unfounded inferences followed that panel discussion in the popular press and in exchanges on the internet. One comment from an internet discussion illustrates some of the naivete at work: "It looks like scientists, with DNA tools, are well on their way to exhaustively knowing where every group of people came from for at least the last 10,000 years."[4] This is neither an accurate assessment of the present situation nor, in fact, is it ever likely to be the case. The human gene pool as a whole is complexly mixed by crosscurrents, eddies, and backwaters. An individual's genes reflect a mere fraction of one's genealogical legacy. Examples repeatedly arise where the phenotype, or outward physical appearance—e.g., skin color, facial features—bear little correspondence to the genotype, or characteristic DNA markers, of an individual. Alternately, recent examples demonstrate that sampled genotypes of populations often reveal little accord with well-documented genealogical records. (See our discussion of the Icelanders in Chapter 9, "Lehi's Footprints.") Many population geneticists have repeatedly reiterated cautionary statements that the complexities of evolutionary genetics make the goal of deciphering population sources and subsequent intermingling of lineages an elusive objective.

The adoption of new scientific techniques and its impact on a discipline has been likened by an anonymous observer to a youth receiving a new telescope for Christmas. "At first, it [the telescope] is enthusiastically turned in all directions, until the owner finds that effective use of the instrument actually requires investing heavily in an increased study of astronomy and mathematics and a discomforting exercise of critical judgment in interpreting what is observed. At that point the initial fervor to apply the tool indiscriminately palls, particularly if some new 'toy' comes on the scene to divert attention. The new toy in human biology and anthropology is DNA analysis. Despite cautions from the best scientists about the limits the new findings have for interpreting human history, some enthusiasts without adequate critical acumen claim too much for DNA study."[5]

The existence of the Book of Mormon as a literary document is a fact. Many hypotheses have been advanced to explain its origin. Those who reject the antiquity of the Book of Mormon assign it a nineteenth-century origin, spawned by the fertile imagination of a simple New York farm boy, or perhaps inspired by the piety of a Campbellite preacher, or imitating the fanciful speculations of an aspiring novelist. Each of these hypotheses has been explored at length elsewhere. Some critics esteem the Book of Mormon as containing worthwhile treatises on issues of ethics and morality but deny its historicity, citing a lack of archeological and genetic corroboration and thereby disparaging its ultimate significance and implications.

At least three major hypotheses can be advanced concerning the Book of Mormon and Native American origins:

1. All Native Americans are of Asian origin. This hypothesis has dominated mainstream science since the sixteenth century.

2. All Native Americans are of Middle Eastern origin. This hypothesis is advocated by some who accept the Book of Mormon account as historical.

3. Most Native Americans are of Asian origin, while a small subset is of Middle Eastern origin but intermingled with the indigenous people. This hypothesis is proposed by others who also accept the historicity of the Book of Mormon. This hypothesis has two alternate subsidiary hypotheses.

  a. No genetic evidence of the Middle Eastern influx has been found yet but will eventually be found given more extensive sampling and analysis.

b.   No genetic evidence of the Middle Eastern influx has been found, and probably never will be found.

Hypotheses 1 and 2 would seem to be testable by direct scientific methods. The genetic constitution of the surviving Native American population has been rather extensively tested. The current data help support the first hypothesis: "All Native Americans are of Asian origin." More precisely, no data have refuted this hypothesis. This latter statement is more accurate concerning the testing of scientific data. Because it is impossible to analyze *all* Native American DNA it is also impossible to unequivocally state that "*All* Native Americans are of Asian origin." Another important consideration concerning this hypothesis is that the present Native American population does not necessarily represent the genetic diversity of pre-Columbian Native American populations.

Clearly the current data refute the second hypothesis: "All Native Americans are of Middle Eastern origin." The data do not indicate an affinity of Native American DNA to that of present-day Middle Eastern populations and certainly do not support a sole origin from that source.

On November 8, 2007, Peggy Fletcher Stack, religion editor for the *Salt Lake Tribune*, reported that the Church of Jesus Christ of Latter day Saints had, in October 2006, changed one word in the introduction to the Book of Mormon, then in a second trade edition with Doubleday of New York. Stack stated, "The book's current introduction, added by the late LDS apostle, Bruce R. McConkie in 1981, includes this statement: 'After thousands of years, all were destroyed except the Lamanites, and they are the principal ancestors of the American Indians.' The new version, seen first in Doubleday's revised edition, reads, 'After thousands of years, all were destroyed except the Lamanites, and they are among the ancestors of the American Indians.'"[6]

We see this wording change as welcome in light of the fact that some who interpret the DNA data as challenging the Book of Mormon's historicity have pointed to this phrase as evidence of factual inaccuracy. They could not use any text in the book itself as the focus of their comments since the Book of Mormon text has never made such a sweeping claim. This change in the introduction now simply provides a better match between the text itself, the introduction, and the genetic evidence to date.

The third hypothesis, which proposes that a small influx to the Native American population was of Middle Eastern origin, specifically ancient Israelite, is more problematic and indeed may not be testable. Why? Because the genetic trace of the remnant of a small population introduced into a much larger population may or may not be detectable, let alone identifiable. Detection of such a link would depend on whether any identifiable distinct genetic markers of the immigrant population were transferred to the much larger resident population and have remained in the surviving population in sufficient frequency to be detected.

Although the principle of parsimony in science states that the simplest explanation is preferred, the simplest explanation is not of necessity the correct one. The simplest explanation is, however, the explanation accepted by science until additional data refute or at least modify it. The DNA data collected to date simply connect Native American populations to specific Asian populations. Therefore, the most parsimonious explanation is an Asian origin for modern Native American peoples. However, when considered in the context of the principles and limitations of population genetics, the data do not exclude the possibility of other gene sources which are not yet detected (or which are simply undetectable) by the limited sampling of currently extant populations. One or more relatively small populations, now extinct or genetically overwhelmed in the gene pool of the Western Hemisphere, could have existed but are no longer evident. The limitations on the potential for data collection and detection mean that some hypotheses of Native American origins simply cannot be tested by DNA research, although other avenues of investigation such as linguistics and archeology may contribute insights. Given the assumptions of a small immigrant colony living in a limited geographical area among a large indigenous population, the necessary tests, based on DNA research, manifestly cannot be designed that would refute the historicity of the

Book of Mormon. Therefore, as stated in Hypothesis 3b, genetic evidence will probably never be discovered that would reveal a small influx of Middle Easterners to Native Americans or that any Native Americans today carry genes that could be linked to such ancestry.

If Hypothesis 1 appears to be corroborated and Hypothesis 2 is clearly refuted, as the current data suggest, then is there any need for additional discussion? What is to be done with Hypothesis 3? We maintain that additional discussion is warranted even though such a hypothesis may be virtually untestable by current scientific means. Our objective in this book is to examine the merits of this third hypothesis, the logical inferences upon which it rests, and its implications for claims about DNA and the Book of Mormon. We intend to examine the genetic and molecular data and explore the recognized limitations to these data, especially the challenge of detecting the infusion of a mere drop of DNA into the extensive gene pool of the ancient Western Hemisphere. We will further discuss the interpretive challenges of population genetics posed by such concepts as bottlenecks, founder effects, genetic drift, and admixture—especially as they relate to Native American populations and the implications for identifying the "children of Lehi," that is, the descendants of peoples mentioned in the Book of Mormon.

Furthermore, we wish to emphasize that, to Latter-day Saints, the ultimate significance of the claims of the Book of Mormon pivots upon the Abrahamic covenant, which states that through Abraham all the nations of the earth will be blessed (Abr. 2:11). This promise extends to the people of the Western Hemisphere through the children of Lehi in essentially the same manner that it applied to the Eastern Hemisphere through the children of Israel generally. The house of Israel has been likened to the leaven of the bread. The leaven is only a small ingredient in the bread, not the bread itself. The children of Lehi can be seen as a spiritual leaven in the same sense that the Abrahamic covenant extended to Israel, leavening the bread that represents the millions of former inhabitants of the New World.[7] Just as the scattering of Israel throughout the Old World has left few or no genetic footprints on the world population, it seems very unlikely that the genetic trace of that leaven will be identified in the New World, let alone detected by DNA research, although its spiritual effects may be very real.

In the final analysis, it is our opinion that the Book of Mormon, like the Bible, is a book of faith. If God proved, without doubt, every whit of the sacred record, then faith, a vital principle, would lose its effect. Hence, our perspective and our motivation for exploring these issues stem mutually from our pursuit of scientific knowledge and understanding as biologists and anthropologists, from our rejection of any over-reaching of interpretation—scientific or scriptural—and from our acceptance of the principle of rational faith in the Book of Mormon.

Notes

[1]D. J. Meldrum and T. D. Stephens, "Who Are the Children of Lehi?" *Journal of Book of Mormon Studies* 12 (2003): 38–51. That paper is an abbreviation of this book, drawing especially on chapter 10.

[2]Sunstone Symposium, Final Program, Salt Lake City, August 2001, 44.

[3]Murphy has since published his manuscript as "Lamanite Genesis, Genealogy, and Genetics," in *American Apocrypha: Essays on the Book of Mormon*, edited by Dan Vogel and Brent Lee Metcalfe (Salt Lake City: Signature Books, 2002), 47–77.

[4]This quotation was taken from an internet exchange that occurred in 1999. We copied the response but without identifying information that would allow retrieval from an archive.

[5]Anonymous, "The Problematic Role of DNA Testing in Unraveling Human History," *Book of Mormon Studies* 9 (2000): 66–74.

[6]Peggy Fletcher Stack, "Minor Edit Stirs Major Ruckus," *Salt Lake Tribune*, A1, A14.

[7]Or as Galatians 3:14 puts it: "That the blessing of Abraham might come on the Gentiles through Jesus Christ; that we might receive the promise of the Spirit through faith."

Chapter Two
A Covenant People: The Bread's Leaven

The Judeo-Christian Bible offers an account of Jehovah's relationship with his chosen, or covenant people up to the meridian of recorded history. Through the patriarchs, we are told, the God of the Old Testament established a covenant with the believing posterity of Adam. That covenant was in turn reestablished with Abraham, promising that his seed should be as numerous as the sands of the sea and that through his descendants all families and all nations of the earth would be blessed" (Abr. 2:11; see also Amos 9:9). Abraham's grandson Jacob had his personal wrestle to know his place with the Lord and received a blessing and a new name: "Israel—Prince that prevails with God."[1] It was written that, when God "separated the sons of Adam, he set the bounds of the people according to the number of the children of Israel" (Deut. 32:8).

The visionary prophet Isaiah measured the span of time largely by the scattering and gathering of the house of Israel. Jesus Christ praised him to the Nephites: "For great are the words of Isaiah. For surely he spake as touching all things concerning my people, which are of the house of Israel" (3 Ne. 23:1-2). Isaiah saw Israel sifted throughout the nations of the world much like leaven in a loaf, dispersing the promises of the covenant and the hope of a Redeemer to the four quarters of the earth. Isaiah foresaw the hosts of Israel eventually gathered and reestablished as a people in the latter days.

From the Israelites' own ethnocentric perspective, they were God's covenant people, occupying center stage in the world drama.

However, from the point of view of their proximate neighbors, let alone the rest of the world, they were a minor, clannish populace that happened to occupy a strategic geographic nexus between two great civilizations, Egypt and Mesopotamia, but were otherwise of little historical consequence. The two greatest kings of Israel, David and Solomon, left hardly a trace in the Middle Eastern archeological record. Yet, rather surprisingly, much of the world certainly has been and continues to be influenced by Israel's history. Perhaps most significantly, the person regarded by a significant fraction of the world's populace as the Savior of humankind was born into the house of Israel. Calendars now turn upon that event. In spite of his pivotal position in history, however, a historical Jesus has been questioned by some modern scholars. In the wake of his crucifixion, the Jewish remnant was scattered, as the kingdoms of Israel and of Judah had been scattered before them. Christians throughout the world reckon time from Jesus's birth and anticipate the apocalyptic times when the Lord will stretch forth his arm to once again gather in His covenant people, the lost sheep of Israel, as a prelude to His return.

In spite of the perception of ethnocentricity and elitism among historical and modern Jews, the original concept of a covenant people is a spiritual and religious construct, not a strictly ethnic or genealogical identity. The covenant binds together all who have accepted the terms of belief and attendant behavior. Those not born into the house of Israel are not automatically excluded but can participate in the covenant through "adoption." For Christians, "they which are of faith . . . are the children of Abraham" (Gal. 3:7). The biblical book of Ruth tells the story of a Moabite woman who was the great-grandmother of David. Ruth uttered these immortal words to her mother-in-law Naomi, "Whither thou goest I will go; and where thou lodgest, I will lodge; thy people shall be my people, and thy God my God" (Ruth 1:16).

From Israel's earliest history, its gene pool was a melting pot of ethnicities and nationalities. For example Joseph, the favored son of Jacob, who became second only to Pharaoh, took an Egyptian wife. Therefore, all of his children, including the favored lineages of Ephraim and Manasseh and their descendants, are of mixed "blood." It also seems very likely that considerable mixing with the Egyptian gene pool occurred during the several centuries that Israelites were enslaved in Egypt. Interestingly, this enslavement, so important in the Hebrew lineage record, can barely be established from Egyptian records and has been denied as a historical occurrence by some modern scholars.

This Joseph, son of Jacob, received an ambiguous patriarchal blessing that he would be "a fruitful bough . . . whose branches run over the wall" (Gen. 49:22), which Mormons interpret to mean that some of his descendants would inherit the land of promise on the other side of the ocean, just as the Book of Mormon describes. Christ himself identified these descendants as the "other sheep" of whom he hinted to the Jews (John 10:16; 3 Ne.15:17, 21). By their account, these descendants heard the voice of the Shepherd and made record of it. The Book of Mormon announces itself as another testament of Christ, bearing record as a voice from the dust of His covenant with this American branch of the house of Israel, transplanted to the Western Hemisphere.

The Book of Mormon narrates the exodus of a small band of Israelites, two families led by Lehi out of the doomed city of Jerusalem in 600 B.C. (One family was descended from Ephraim, the other from Manasseh; but they also called themselves Jews because they lived in Jerusalem.) They journeyed through the wilderness and across the sea to make a new home in their promised land, which we now identify as the Americas. From two of Lehi's sons and their adherents, arose two principal societies, or more accurately cultures— the Nephites and the Lamanites—who occupy center stage in a drama fraught with wars and contentions. We use "cultures" advisedly, not "lineages." They were cultural-political-religious groups, not necessarily restricted to particular lineal descent, which soon encompassed varied populations, some made mention of and, very likely, some that went largely or completely unmentioned. Within the first generation after their arrival in the New World, Jacob, the younger brother of Nephi, had already reduced the distinction between Lamanites and Nephites to the basis of allegiance. The Nephites were distinguished as those who were friendly toward Nephi, the Christian prophet of the covenant; those who sought to destroy the Nephites were called Lamanites (Jacob 1:13–14; see also vv. 6–8). Inclusion within the covenant was not restricted to any specific lineage but included all who accepted the terms of the covenant. Adherents to the covenant were always a minority. In contrast, dissenters felt no compunction about freely mingling with other nonbelievers.

A curious aspect of the Book of Mormon is the occasional pointed declaration by a prominent character that he is a direct descendant of Lehi (e.g., Alma 10:3, 3 Ne. 5:20). They would apparently be stating the obvious, unless such statements were an implicit acknowledgement that Lehi's posterity was mingling with others in the region. Nephi, the record keeper, had already set the convention of relative silence about the presence of others from the time the family left Jerusalem, long before they set sail for the New World. Without doubt, indigenous people had settled at the oases along the Frankincense Trail the length of the Arabian Peninsula. Those springs were crucial to the survival of Lehi's little band sojourning in the desert; yet during their eight years' travel to the land Bountiful (from which they embarked on their transoceanic voyage), in all of the negotiations for passage, water, and supplies, Nephi never once mentions interactions with local people. Is it therefore surprising that the tradition continued by not directly mentioning the indigenous people certainly present in the New World? Hugh Nibley, BYU professor of ancient scripture, remarked, "Strictly speaking, the Book of Mormon is the history of a group of sectaries preoccupied with their own religious affairs, who only notice the presence of other groups when they have reason to mingle or collide with them. . . . There is nothing whatever in the Book of Mormon to indicate that everything that is found in the New World before Columbus must be either Nephite or Lamanite."[2]

Thus, the Book of Mormon record is significantly restricted in scope and conveys only a limited sense of the various peoples' enterprises and expansions. For example, in the days of the Nephite King Benjamin, everyone over whom he reigned (constituting all of the Nephites) were within a mere day's journey from the tower from which Benjamin addressed them only one day after sending out a proclamation for them to gather (Mosiah 1:10). In contrast, the mighty city of Nineveh, to whom the Old Testament prophet Jonah preached, had perhaps 120,000 residents and required a three-day journey to traverse (Jonah 3:3).

Ultimately, Nephite culture was corrupted from within and overwhelmed from without; and the remaining Nephites were virtually hunted to extinction but not before hiding up a record. And yet, this brief synopsis, so familiar to Latter-day Saints, does little to convey the convoluted history, complexities, and extent of the cultural, political, and genealogical relationships of thousands of generations of Book of Mormon peoples. It fails to acknowledge the subtle but persistent allusions to the more expansive stage and larger cast of characters just beyond the immediate preoccupations of the record keeper, who lacked the benefit of modern transportation and communications that we take for granted.

At the same time, the simplified synopsis presented here fails to emphasize the focus of the record keeper. It glosses over the central message and primary purpose of the Book of Mormon, which indeed have a potentially greater scope and farther-reaching influence. That purpose is "to show unto the remnant of the house of Israel what great things the Lord hath done for their fathers; that they might know the covenants of the Lord . . . to the convincing of Jew and Gentile that Jesus is the Christ, the Eternal God."[3] The focus is on the covenant—the leaven in the bread.

Notes

[1]William Smith, *A Dictionary of the Bible* (Grand Rapids, Mich.: Zondervan Publishing House, 1948), *s.v.* Jacob.

[2]Hugh Nibley, *Since Cumorah*, Vol. 7 of THE COLLECTED WORKS OF HUGH NIBLEY (1964; rpt., Salt Lake City: Deseret Book/Provo, Utah: Foundation for Ancient Research and Mormon Studies, 1988).

[3]Book of Mormon, title page.

Chapter Three
Clerics, Latter-day Saints, and Lamanites

When Columbus landed in the Americas, he didn't initially question the existence of people in the New World because he didn't consider that America was a *new* world. Rather, he saw it as an eastern approach to Asia—hence the label "Indians" for Native Americans. Christian Europe accepted that all people were initially descended from the family of Adam and Eve and, secondly, from the family of Noah. But once the distinctness and isolation of the Americas became apparent the question arose for scholars and clerics alike: What was the Indians' origin? If they were not descended from Adam and Noah, then perhaps they were not to be counted among humanity. This attitude helped justify a great deal of the inhumane treatment that colonizing European nations inflicted on indigenous peoples of the Americas. On the other hand, if these people *were* part of the human family and possessed human souls that should be claimed for Christianity, then where did they come from? How did they come to be in this New World?

For the Native Americans themselves, there is no mystery surrounding their origins. With few exceptions, they have maintained that they didn't come "from" anywhere but were created by the Great Spirit right here in their own native land. For people outside the Native American community, however, theories of Indian origins have abounded and have included fantastic propositions—for example, that they were survivors from the fabled Atlantis. Less fantastic, but considered highly improbable, has been the suggestion that they descended from ancient seafarers from Egypt, Phoenicia, China, Australia, or Africa. In short, nearly every possible source of immigration, fanciful or otherwise, has been considered at some time or other.

A notion popularly entertained in the sixteenth through nineteenth centuries was that Native Americans were the remnants of the lost tribes of Israel, who marched off the biblical stage and out of history following the Assyrian captivity about 721 B.C. According to anthropologist Thomas Dale Stewart Jr., "The [Catholic] Church of 16th century Europe accepted the New World inhabitants as the descendants of the Lost Tribes. In support of this biblically derived explanation, scholars and theologians of the time searched for cultural parallels between the contemporary Jews and the Amerindians."[1]

Numerous early publications explored these beliefs. For example, James Adair's 1775 *The History of the American Indians* listed twenty-three parallels between Indian and Jewish customs. He claimed that Indians spoke a corrupt form of Hebrew, honored the Jewish Sabbath, performed circumcision, and offered animal sacrifice. Manasseh ben Israel's *The Hope of Israel* (1652, 1792) includes the claim that a remnant of the lost ten tribes had been discovered in Peru. Samuel Sewall's *Phaenomena Quaedam Apocalyptica* (1697, 1727) suggested that the Indians are Israelites, that America might be the place of the New Jerusalem, and that the other sheep mentioned in John 10:16 are the American Indians.[2] Solomon Spaulding's *Manuscript Found* (1885), and Ethan Smith's *A View of the Hebrews* (1825) explore later variants of these hypotheses.

Some critics have mistakenly assumed that the Book of Mormon likewise identifies the lost tribes of Israel as ancestors of the American Indians. Although the Book of Mormon does deal with a small group of Israelites, it does not identify the Native Americans as the lost tribes but rather as descendants of the "Lamanites," a people likely drawn from several sources, one of which was Joseph of Egypt, a son of Jacob/Israel. The common belief held at one time by most members of the Church of Jesus Christ of Latter-day Saints and probably still assumed by many is that *all* Native Americans are Lamanites, interpreted in this instance as the direct descendants of the rebellious sons of Lehi.

On June 4, 1834, Joseph Smith stated in a letter to his wife Emma as he traveled across Illinois: "The whole of our journey [we have been] wandering over the plains of the Nephites, recounting occasionally the history of the Book of Mormon, roving over the mounds of that once beloved people of the Lord, picking up their skulls and their bones as a proof of its divine authenticity."[3] This letter suggests Joseph Smith's early belief that, at least in Illinois, the mounds and bones he and his party encountered were those of Nephites. Historian Kenneth Godfrey concludes: "After their arrival in the Great Basin, most church members it appears believed that Nephite history was large enough to accommodate the whole hemisphere."[4] Because the Book of Mormon does indeed describe a "land northward" and a "land southward" connected by a "narrow neck of land," the briefest glance at a globe explains how readily a hemispheric model would take root. We were both raised with this traditional understanding, like most other members of the Church.

However, a historical review of this notion reveals it for what it is—the speculation of individuals in the absence of an authoritative position.[5] Even today, the common perception among most Latter-day Saints is that the Indians of North and South America whom the first Europeans encountered are remnants of Book of Mormon peoples. Recent informed opinions, however, that include insights from contemporary archeological and anthropological findings are actually more harmonious with the historical account presented by the Book of Mormon text itself.[6]

Most members of the Church realize that the peoples mentioned in the Book of Mormon were diverse. Specific reference is made to three immigrations: (1) an early group of Semites dispersed from the Tower of Babel, the "Jaredites"; (2) a party of Israelites, principally from the tribe of Judah, "the people of Zarahemla," sometimes called the Mulekites; and (3) the third, almost contemporary with the Mulekites, consisting of Lehi's and Ishmael's families, representing the tribes of Ephraim and Manasseh. Although the Book of Mormon deals primarily with the Nephites and Lamanites, both descended from Lehi, his posterity was actually much more complex. During the centuries before Christ, the Nephites had been divided into four groups: Nephites, Jacobites, Josephites, and Zoramites. The Lamanites in turn had been divided into three such lineages: Lamanites, Lemuelites, and Ishmaelites. Thus, there were at least seven named lineages specifically mentioned. These lineages are listed in three different places in the Nephite record, and they are always given in precisely the same order (Jacob 1:13, 4 Ne. 1:36–38, Morm. 1:8). Doctrine and Covenants 3:16–18, a revelation given in 1828, lists the seven a fourth time. (The Book of Mormon text never uses the term "Mulekites.")

The Jacobites and Josephites were named for Nephi's younger brothers who were born during the eight years that the family spent in the Arabian wilderness. The Zoramites were named after the servant of Laban, who was adopted as a member of Lehi's party, although his ethnicity is never mentioned. The Lamanites and Lemuelites were named after Nephi's older brothers, while the Ishmaelites were descended from the sons of Ishmael and their wives, whose ethnic backgrounds are also never mentioned. Ishmael's daughters became wives to Lehi's sons. These lineages apparently maintained a degree of recognition throughout the record, although Jacob established very early the convention of referring to the Lamanites generically as all those who collectively fought against the people friendly to Nephi. Note this distinction— not merely the descendants of Nephi, but "the *people* friendly to Nephi" (Jacob 1:13–14).

In the wake of the cataclysms recorded in the Western Hemisphere at the time of Christ's crucifixion at Jerusalem, the survivors mentioned in the narrative were, without individual family distinction, singularly united. For nearly 200 years after the coming of Christ to the Americas, there were no Lamanites "nor any manner of -ites; but they were in one, the children of Christ, and heirs to the kingdom of God" (4 Ne. 1:17). Soon, however, a part of the people fell away and took upon themselves the name Lamanites;

"therefore there began to be Lamanites again in the land" (4 Ne. 1:20). Clearly, "Lamanite" in this case refers to the anti-Christian faction, as perceived by the keepers of the record. These later Lamanites were even less a genealogical group than the earlier ones. They consisted of a mixture of descendants of Lehi, Ishmael, Zoram, and Mulek, the people of Zarahemla, likely even Jaredites, and also "all that had become Lamanites because of their dissensions" (D&C 10:48). From the point of view of the Nephite record keepers and defenders of the Christian faith, these dissenters would likely encompass any indigenous populations that were not counted among the members of the church of Christ or that did not demonstrate allegiance to the Nephite system of government. This "them-versus-us" concept is somewhat like the monikers of "Jew and Gentile."

After the apostasy around A.D. 200, the seven lineages once more came into distinction. Just how true these affiliations were to genealogical relations after two centuries of ostensible unification is unknown. Today, few people have a sense of their specific genealogy beyond their grandparents or great-grandparents, let alone their family roots of two hundred years ago. The situation would be even more extreme in a homogeneous, largely illiterate society, without surnames. Naturally the possibility of clannish or tribal alignments must be born in mind, but such affiliations would not necessarily be restricted to strict lineage. Even after this apostasy and the reemergence of "–ites," the collective term "Nephite" applied to the followers of Christ, while "Lamanite" applied to nonbelievers, irrespective of their lineage. This dichotomy was clearly a religious-political distinction, not a lineage designation.

Early LDS references to the American Indians commonly referred to them collectively as Lamanites. What various connotations does the label "Lamanite" carry? The word has been used in at least five different ways: (1) A lineage descended through male lines from Laman, Lehi's oldest son; (2) A pre-Christian nation descended from Laman and his original followers, i.e., the Lamanites, the Lemuelites, and the Ishmaelites, and possibly other adherents, who were enemies of the Nephites; (3) The "later

Lamanites" after A.D. 194 an anti-Christian cultural-political group, not based on ethnicity; (4) descendants of all seven lineages as they exist at present—the entire posterity of Lehi, Ishmael, and Zoram, as well as of Mulek and his associates, possibly even with remnants of the Jaredites; (5) all American Indians collectively (often including the Polynesians).

In 1975, Lane Johnson, a member of the *Ensign* staff, wrote "Who and Where Are the Lamanites?"[7] in an effort to map Lamanite distribution. As Johnson notes, this was no simple task and it depended on the precise meaning assigned to the label itself. As indicated above, "Lamanite" referred initially to genealogy but within two or three generations had shifted to mean a religious-political faction whose distinguishing feature was its opposition to the church of Christ. Lineage became an increasingly minor factor.

Several statements by LDS General Authorities, past and present, have acknowledged the dispersal of "Lehi's children" among other inhabitants of the Americas.[8] As early as 1929, long before DNA was even identified as the cell's genetic material, President Anthony W. Ivins, of the First Presidency, delivered a general conference address advocating restraint about theories on Book of Mormon geography: "There has never been anything yet set forth that definitively settles the question. So the Church says we are just waiting until we discover the truth." He added an even more significant acknowledgement: "It [the Book of Mormon] does not tell us that no one was here before them [the Book of Mormon peoples]. It does not tell us that people did not come after."[9] Elder Mark E. Petersen of the Council of the Twelve wrote, "As the ancient Israelites suffered a dispersion which sprinkled them among all the nations, so the descendants of Laman and Lemuel were sifted over the vast areas of the western hemisphere. They are found from pole to pole."[10] Elder Spencer W. Kimball, also an apostle, qualified "Lamanite" as including, "all Indians *and Indian mixtures*, such as the Polynesians, the Guatemalans, the Peruvians, as well as the Sioux, the Apache, the Mohawk, the Navajo, and others. It is a large group of great people."[11] Such statements indicate that these Church leaders did not exclude the likelihood that Book of Mormon peoples had mixed with other populations. More recently, Elder Dallin H. Oaks of the Quorum of the Twelve has reiterated that "the Book of Mormon is not the history of all of the people that have lived on the continents of North and South America in all ages. . . . It only purports to be an account of a few peoples who inhabited a portion of the Americas during a few millennia."[12]

Some people have pointed to the addition of the anonymously authored "Introduction" to the 1981 edition of the Book of Mormon as confirming the assumption that all Native Americans are exclusively descended from the "Lamanites." After a brief and simplified synopsis of the origin and identity of populations depicted in the record, that introduction states: "After thousands of years, all were destroyed except the Lamanites, and they are the principal ancestors of the American Indians."[13] There are actually two ways to view this statement. First, one might consider this introduction as a commentary added to the scripture to aid the reader but not, in itself, canonized as scripture any more than, say, the "Bible Dictionary" in the 1979 LDS edition of the Bible. The second way to view the "Introduction" is to consider it written or approved under inspiration. The introduction itself gives no information relevant for distinguishing between these two views. The introduction may reflect the long-held assumption of many Latter-day Saints that the Book of Mormon renders an account of *all* the ancient inhabitants of the Americas—who may be presumed to have descended from the Lamanites. This assumption seems to have been refuted by the DNA evidence, disclaimed by numerous General Authorities, and definitively replaced by new wording, operationalized in October 2006, identifying Lamanites as "among the ancestors" of Native Americans. (See discussion, pp. 5–6.)

Consequently, the term "Lamanite," as used in the introduction, implies the broader meaning, originally established by Jacob early in the record itself, referring to all the nonbelievers who fought against the Nephites throughout the Book of Mormon record. By the time Mormon and Moroni were preparing their abridgments of the record, "Lamanite" clearly served as a cultural/ political label for those who either stood apart from or openly opposed the Nephite religion and government. By the time Moroni sealed up his record, as far as he was concerned, all who remained in his world were Lamanites or non-Christians, regardless of their nationality or genealogical affinities. His reference to the annihilation of his people was not merely a corpse count but also a recognition that any who survived had affiliated with the Lamanite religious-political system. In effect, everyone remaining in the Western Hemisphere (insofar as he comprehended it) was from his perspective, a "Lamanite." In that broader sense, calling Native Americans descendants of Lamanites presents no inconsistency with the genetic data. In A.D. 421 when the record was sealed up, the people Moroni would have recognized as "Lamanites"—no matter what their actual ethnic origin might have been—were indeed ancestors of the modern American Indians.

Early Latter-day Saints may have over-generalized and oversimplified the inference that the American Indians were *exclusively* the literal descendants of the Book of Mormon peoples. Given the limited knowledge of New World history, archeology, and population genetics at that time, these simplified interpretations should not be surprising. When these early inferences are considered in the context of the early Saints' beliefs and emphasis on the doctrine of the scattering of Israel among all nations, they are even less surprising.

We should recognize that the Book of Mormon is a severe abridgment of a history spanning thousands of years. The record emphasizes religious events of significance to a single segment of a diverse population. The tendency is to oversimplify an already abbreviated story-line for the sake of conveying its theological doctrines—clearly the point most vital to Mormon as editor. In the wake of this oversimplification, the secular significance of "Lamanites" as a historical label often goes unappreciated. This development has led to further unfounded generalizations, which unavoidably collide with recent discoveries about the complex origins and history of Native Americans.

As a matter of particular concern, some critics have interpreted the lack of DNA evidence connecting Native Americans to

Middle Eastern origins as refuting the claim that "Lamanites" are among the ancestors of the American Indians. Anthropologist Thomas W. Murphy concludes: "DNA has lent no support to the traditional Mormon belief about the origins of Native Americans. . . . [T]o date no intimate genetic link has been found between ancient Israelites and indigenous Americans."[15] In fact, we agree with this conclusion. If the Mormon "belief" referred to in the preceding statement is that all pre-Columbian inhabitants of the Americas are exclusive descendants of the principal peoples mentioned in the Book of Mormon, then it is accurate to say that the DNA data lend no obvious support to that assumption.

Yet this position is in itself an oversimplification. In July 28, 1996, two college students watching hydroplane races on the Columbia River near Kennewick, Washington, discovered a human skull 9300–9600 years old. The antiquity of the skull with "Caucasoid" features ignited a firestorm that has continued for the past ten years. Was there an earlier population of inhabitants that predated modern Native Americans? One that did not have close ties to modern Asiatic populations? What might be the historical, let alone political, ramifications of such a revelation? The Umatilla Indians of the Columbia River Basin, the tribe located closest to the discovery, immediately laid claim to the remains as those of an ancestor and completely dismissed scientific claims and issues: "Our elders have taught us that once a body goes into the ground, it is meant to stay there until the end of time," commented Armand Minthorn, a tribal religious leader, in a written statement.

If this individual is truly over 9,000 years old, that only substantiates our belief that he is Native American. From our oral histories, we know that our people have been part of this land since the beginning of time. We do not believe that our people migrated here from another continent, as the scientists do. . . . Scientists believe that because the individual's head measurement does not match ours, he is not Native American. Our elders have told us that Indian people did not always look the way we look today. Some scientists say that if this individual is not studied further, we, as Indians, will be destroying evidence of our history. We already know our history. It is passed on to us through our elders and through our religious practices.[16]

To the degree that Minthorn is speaking for his tribe, the Umatillas don't want scientific theories or anything else, including the Book of Mormon story, which teaches that at least some of the people living in America came from the Middle East or, more importantly, that through the Abrahamic covenant they are entitled to the blessings of the gospel.

Do we want to spend our energy pitting our LDS oral histories, which may stray beyond the claims of the Book of Mormon itself, against the oral histories of the Native Americans, while we both ignore the data coming out of the earth? (D&C 88:79) Folklore and tradition may easily—in fact, almost inevitably will—run afoul of fact if definitions and limitations, such as what constitutes a "Lamanite," are not judiciously observed and respected. Similarly, overinterpreting available scientific data may also obscure truth, as history has repeatedly revealed.

The notion that LDS oral history and tradition have strayed beyond the Book of Mormon story is demonstrated in the 1981 statement in the Introduction that the Lamanites were the "principal" ancestors of the American Indians. The rewording in October 2006 that the Lamanites "are among the ancestors of the American Indians" brings that introduction more in line with what probably actually occurred historically.

Notes

[1]T. D. Stewart, *The People of America* (New York: Scribners, 1973).

[2]Described in ibid.

[3]Kenneth W. Godfrey, "What Is the Significance of Zelph in the Study of Book of Mormon Geography?" *Journal of Book of Mormon Studies* 8 (1999): 73.

[4]Ibid., 76.

[5]Matthew Roper, "Limited Geography and the Book of Mormon:

Historical Antecedents and Early Interpretations," *FARMS Review* 16 (2004): 225–75.

[6]John E. Clark, "Archeology, Relics, and Book of Mormon Belief," *Journal of Book of Mormon Studies* 14 (2005): 38–49.

[7]Lane Johnson, "Who and Where Are the Lamanites?" *Ensign*, December 1975, 15.

[8]For a thorough review of these co-inhabitants of the Western Hemisphere, see Matthew Roper, "Nephi's Neighbors: Book of Mormon Peoples and Pre-Columbian Populations," *FARMS Review* 15 (2003): 91–128.

[9]Anthony W. Ivins, *Conference Report* (Salt Lake City: Church of Jesus Christ of Latter-day Saints, April 1929), 15–16.

[10]Mark E. Petersen, *Children of Promise* (Salt Lake City: Bookcraft, 1981), 31.

[11]Spencer W. Kimball, "Of Royal Blood," *Ensign*, July 1971, 7; emphasis ours.

[12]Dallin H. Oaks, "The Historicity of the Book of Mormon," address at the Foundation for Ancient Research and Mormon Studies dinner, Provo, Utah, October 29, 1993, http://farms.byu.edu/display.php?id =30&table=transcripts (accessed October 30, 2007).

[13]Introduction, *The Book of Mormon: Another Testament of Christ* (Salt Lake City: Church of Jesus Christ of Latter-day Saints, 1981), introduction not paginated.

[14]Thomas W. Murphy, "Lamanite Genesis, Genealogy, and Genetics," in *American Apocrypha: Essays on the Book of Mormon*, edited by Dan Vogel and Brent Lee Metcalfe (Salt Lake City: Signature Books, 2002), 48.

[15]Armand Minthorn, written statement, quoted in Douglas Preston, "The Lost Man," *New Yorker*, June 16, 1997, 74.

Chapter Four
Sharpening Occam's Razor

The general public's perception of how science proceeds is often very different from reality. This perception may encompass a considerable spectrum of ideas. Some see science rather pessimistically as a rudderless ship, constantly reinventing itself with each new "revolutionary" discovery. Others may view science somewhat ideally as the only reliable method for making sense of life's experiences, and they may attribute value only to conclusions that are "scientifically tested." Indeed, the scientific method has been an enormously successful approach to comprehending a complex world. The tremendous strides in our understanding of nature, increased standard of living, improvements in health care, and advances in our ability to create and share information all attest to the success of this method of expanding our knowledge base.

However, in principle, science is not able to prove anything. There are simply too many possibilities to test (if, indeed, an experiment could even be designed to conduct the necessary tests of a hypothesis) to entirely exclude the possibility of a negative outcome. Many hypotheses by their very nature cannot be tested under present circumstances, due either to unrecoverable data or to our present inability to detect them. The object of scientific inquiry is to develop testable hypotheses. Science advances by eliminating incorrect testable hypotheses. By demonstrating a contradictory result, a particular hypothesis can be rejected or falsified. Due to this limitation, science, by its very nature, is always tentative, even though a great deal of confidence can be placed in a hypothesis bolstered by repeated affirmative evidence.

The fact that a hypothesis is not testable does not mean that it is incorrect. It merely means that the data required to evaluate the hypothesis are not available or are not repeatable. The existence of God is a prime example. Although this hypothesis is untestable scientifically, many people, including many scientists would not reject it as false, merely unscientific.

Scientists themselves must occasionally be reminded of and reflect upon the scope and limitations of their craft. To this end, Jeff distributes to idealistic students a tongue-in-cheek set of "cardinal rules" that are, notwithstanding, appropriate to reflect on prior to forging ahead with a scientific investigation. Three of these cautionary adages have relevance to the subject at hand.

1. For every complex problem, there is a solution that is simple, neat, and wrong.

2. The absence of evidence does not constitute evidence of absence.

3. Proving that a particular process can produce a given result is not the same as proving that only that process can produce the result.

The first of these adages points out that simple explanations often fail to fully account for the complexities of answers to some of life's questions, such as the prehistory of human populations. Generalizations may appear neat and tidy but often gloss over complicating details and thus fail to deliver a complete explanation. Nature rarely follows what we perceive as the shortest path. The adage makes back-handed reference to blind reliance on parsimony, a principle in science asserting that the simplest answer is always the preferred answer. For example, in cladistics (a method for testing hypotheses about the descent relationships among populations), the preferred family tree is the simplest one, i.e., the one that requires the fewest intermediate steps. This principle goes back at least as far as Aristotle who wrote, "Nature operates in the shortest way possible."[1] But the contemporary version of this philosophical approach to scientific questions traces its roots primarily to the fourteenth-century logician and Franciscan friar William of Occam (or Ockham). Occam was a village in the English county of Surrey where William was born. The principle simply states: "Entities should not be multiplied unnecessarily."[2]

This parsimonious approach is often phrased as: "When you have two competing hypotheses, which make exactly the same predictions, the simpler one is the better." This adage is referred to as "Occam's Razor." Many scientists have adopted or reinvented Occam's Razor, as when Isaac Newton stated, as a rule: "We are to admit no more causes of natural things than such as are both true and sufficient to explain their appearances."[3] Occam's Razor is used to metaphorically cut away metaphysical concepts, such as Newton's conclusion that God's existence cannot be deduced by reason alone. That one didn't make him very popular with the pope, but it acknowledged the nonscientific nature of the hypothesis.

As an example of Occam's Razor, Einstein's theory of special relativity is preferred over Lorentz's theory that rulers contract and clocks slow down when in motion through the "ether" (an imperceptible substance once believed to fill the apparent void of space). Einstein's equations for transforming space-time are the same as Lorentz's equations for transforming rulers and clocks, but Einstein recognized that ether could not be detected; therefore, it was more parsimonious to eliminate it from the equation.[4]

Stephen Hawking explains in *A Brief History of Time*: "We could still imagine that there is a set of laws that determines events completely for some supernatural being, who could observe the present state of the universe without disturbing it. However, such models of the universe are not of much interest to us mortals. It seems better to employ the principle known as Occam's Razor and cut out all the features of the theory which cannot be observed."[5] But the nonexistence of either the ether or of a supernatural being cannot be deduced through the application of Occam's Razor alone.

Currently, Occam's Razor is often cited in stronger forms than Occam ever intended, as can be seen in some of the following examples taken from various textbooks:

If you have two equally likely solutions to a problem, pick the simplest.

If you have two theories which both explain the observed facts, then you should use the simplest until more evidence comes along.

The simplest explanation for some phenomenon is more likely to be accurate than more complicated explanations.

The explanation requiring the fewest assumptions is most likely to be correct.

As these quotations show, the impact of the basic principle has been successively expanded. Initially, Occam's Razor was used to order hypotheses that predicted the same result. In the later iterations, parsimony has become a rule for determining which alternate hypothesis is more probably correct. That is not what Occam intended. The principle of parsimony should be viewed as a heuristic rule-of-thumb, a convention that indicates which hypothesis to test first. Science advances through elimination by refutation. The simplest hypothesis, if incorrect, is most readily refuted, prompting the researcher to advance to the next simplest, and so on. But some people apply it as if it is an axiom of scientific validation: The simplest explanation is most likely to be correct. That is not necessarily the case. The Razor doesn't tell us anything about a hypothesis's truth. Indeed, examples from the biological sciences repeatedly illustrate that things often turn out to be much more complicated than anticipated. The principle of parsimony alone should never be relied upon to draw or ultimately defend a conclusion.

In historical and descriptive sciences, the ability to experimentally test alternate hypotheses may be limited by the data available or even attainable. For the archeologist or the paleontologist, tests of hypotheses are constrained by the often serendipitous discovery of artifacts and fossils. For the population geneticist, tests are limited by the current make-up of the gene pool of modern populations and by the ability to adequately sample representative individuals. The modern population is the product of generations of mutation, natural selection, bottlenecks, genetic drift, and admixture, and is unavoidably very different than the ancestral population's genetic makeup. In light of these sampling limitations, it must be remembered that the absence of detected evidence does not equate with evidence of absence, as proposed in Adage No. 2.

The revolution in population studies has been catapulted forward by the ability to sequence long stretches of the nucleotides (A, T, C, and G's) that make up DNA. But this ability provides only raw data that are subsequently subjected to interpretation. The process of mutation leaves some clues about the sequence of transpired events but eliminates others. The random nature of many of these events means that there is the potential—in fact, the likelihood—that a single element in the sequence may have been affected multiple times down through the history of the lineage. Each subsequent change may erase part of the record of preceding events. In applying parsimony to the analysis of DNA sequences, researchers impose the assumption that history has pursued the simplest course—i.e., the course that requires the fewest number of mutation steps. One implication of this procedure is the assumption that, if two lineages share the same mutation, they most likely inherited it from a common ancestor. This assumption requires fewer steps than the counter-assumption that the lineages evolved the mutation independently and separately.

However, demonstrating that a particular process can produce a result is not the same as proving that only that process can produce that result—Adage No. 3. There are ample examples of nature solving challenging problems in similar but independent ways, even when arriving at a common end point. This process is called convergence. In some instances, the distinctions are obvious—for example, achieving flight by means of feathers (birds) as opposed to a skin membrane (bats). In others, they are subtler, as the mechanism of tongue protrusion among some frogs and salamanders. In still others, it is effectively impossible to recognize, as in point mutations (alterations in a single base pair) in DNA sequences. The present state of a nucleotide in the sequence tells the researcher nothing directly about the history of that site, only its current status. Molecular biologists who study genealogical relationships based on sequence analysis may find that their hypothetical tree has to accommodate a large degree of convergence to explain the present pattern of the sequences. Yet these convergences only become apparent and can be tentatively resolved only when large sets of pooled data are considered to arrive at an inferred consensus—a compromise among alternate hypotheses.

In summary, science generates tentative explanations derived from interpretations of the limited observations at hand. Testing hypotheses should proceed in an orderly fashion from the simplest to the more complex, without assuming that the simpler explanation has more likelihood of being correct. These hypotheses are constrained by the inherent or circumstantial limitations of the data. The more limited the data, the larger the assumptions, and the more tentatively the hypotheses derived from them must be phrased. The simple absence of data cannot falsify a hypothesis, but neither does it corroborate it. We'd expect that the interpretation of complex biological processes, especially their historical traces, will be particularly tentative and subject to frequent revision. This is certainly the case in the study of DNA and human population genetics.

Notes

[1] This statement was likely derived by Robert Grosseteste from Book 5 of Aristotle's *Physics (De Lineis, Angulis et Figuris)*. See Anne Jackson Fremantle, *Age of Belief: The Medieval Philosophers* (Boston: Houghton Mifflin, 1955), 202.

[2] W. M. Thorburn, "Occam's Razor," *Mind* 24 (1915): 287–88.

[3] Isaac Newton, *Principia: Mathematical Principles of Natural Philosophy* (Berkeley: University of California Press, 1999), 791.

[4] Thorburn, "Occam's Razor," 287–88.

[5] Stephen W. Hawking, *A Brief History of Time: From Big Bang to Black Holes* (Toronto: Bantam Books, 1988), 55.

Chapter Five
The DNA Revolution

Genetics is the study of heredity—the characteristics that off-spring inherit from their parents. A person's genetic makeup large-ly determines his or her physical characteristics and abilities. The genetic material is deoxyribonucleic acid (DNA). DNA and associ-ated proteins can be seen in a stained cell under a microscope as densely stained bodies called chromosomes. There are 46 total chromosomes in all the cells of the body except the sex cells.

The 23 pairs of chromosomes are divided into 22 pairs of autosomal chromosomes (autosomes are all the chromosomes except the sex chromosomes) and one pair of sex chromosomes, which determines the sex of the individual. The autosomal pairs are numbered 1 through 22, and the sex chromosomes are designated as X or Y chromosomes. A normal female has two X chromosomes (XX), while a normal male has one X and one Y chromosome (XY). When a sperm cell and an egg cell fuse during fertilization, each contributes 23 chromosomes to the offspring. As a result, half of an individual's genetic makeup comes from the father and half from the mother. Sperm cells contribute little more than chromo-somes to the mating, whereas the oocyte is a complete cell, except that it has only half a complement of chromosomes. As a result, the new individual receives all its cellular structures from the mother, including the mitochondria. The mitochondria are the powerhous-es of the cell and contain their own DNA, called mitochondrial DNA (mtDNA). Generally, all the mtDNA is inherited from an individual's mother.

When a sperm cell fertilizes an egg cell, the sperm cell's chromosomes determine the individual's sex. If a sperm cell carries a Y chromosome, a male results; but if a sperm cell carries an X chromosome, a female results. Because of inheritance patterns, males receive their Y chromosomes from their fathers, who receive them from their fathers, and so on for thousands of generations. In other words, Y chromosomes are inherited paternally. Both males and females receive their mtDNA from their mothers, who receive them from their mothers, who receive them from their mothers, and so on for thousands of generations. In other words, mtDNA is inherited maternally.

The 22 pairs of autosomal chromosomes are inherited from both mother and father. The offspring receives one member of each chromosome pair from the father and one from the mother, but the specific member from each parent's pair of chromosomes is randomly determined. There is no segregation of maternal versus paternal chromosomes. They are shuffled in each generation, being randomly inherited from the grandparents, the great-grandparents, and so on for thousands of generations. To introduce further variation into the offspring's genotype, the homologous chromosome pairs undergo recombination. During recombination, portions of the maternal and paternal members of the chromosome pairs may exchange portions of DNA. The resulting sex cell then has a unique mosaic of both paternal and maternal genes. An example of this mosaic would be a person inheriting his nose shape from his paternal grandfather and his eye color from his maternal grandmother.

The functional unit of heredity is the gene. Each gene is a segment of DNA in a chromosome, but not necessarily a continuous stretch of DNA. Each chromosome contains any number of genes, from a few to a few thousand. All of the genes are collectively called the genome. The genome of a person is responsible for that person's genetic traits. The genes on a given chromosome tend to pass from parent to child as a "linkage group." That is, those genes tend to be inherited as a group rather than individually.

Both chromosomes of a pair contain similar but not necessarily identical genes. The genes at the same locus on paired chromosomes are called alleles. If allelic genes are identical, the person is homozygous for the trait specified by that gene. If the two alleles are different, the person is heterozygous for the trait. Within a population, specific genes may be represented by multiple alleles occurring in varied frequencies.

Medical science is aware of human genetic traits because defective alleles for those traits exist in the population. For example, a gene on chromosome 11 helps make the pigment responsible for skin, hair, and eye color. The normal allele for the gene produces a normal pigment. An abnormal allele, however, produces little or no pigment. If a person inherits two defective alleles of the gene, a homozygous condition, that person lacks normal pigment in the skin, hair, and eyes. This condition is referred to as albinism.

For many genetic traits, the effects of one allele can mask the effect of another allele for the same trait. For example, a person who is heterozygous for the pigment gene on chromosome 11 has a normal pigment gene on one chromosome 11 and a defective gene for pigment on the other chromosome 11. One copy of the pigment gene is enough to make normal pigment. As a result, the person who is heterozygous appears normal. The allele that produces the normal pigment is said to be dominant, whereas the allele producing the abnormal pigment is recessive. The lost function of the defective allele is masked by the dominant, normal allele. However, the defective allele hasn't gone away and may be carried into later generations; if it becomes associated with another recessive allele of the same gene in a fertilized egg, then that child will have albinism.

Dominant traits are represented by uppercase letters, and recessive traits are represented by lowercase letters. In the example of albinism, "A" represents the dominant normal, pigmented condition and "a" the recessive albino condition. The possible combinations of dominant and recessive alleles for normal pigment versus albinism are AA (homozygous dominant), Aa (heterozygous), and aa (homozygous recessive). The pair of alleles that a person has for a given trait is called the genotype. The person's appearance is called the phenotype. A person with the genotype AA or Aa has the phenotype of normal pigmentation, whereas a person with the genotype aa has the phenotype of albinism. If an albino person (aa) mates with a heterozygous normal person (Aa), the probability is that half of their children will be albino (aa) and half will be normal heterozygous carriers (Aa). If two carriers (Aa) mate, the probability is that 1 in 4 offspring will be homozygous dominant (AA), 1 in 4 will be homozygous recessive (aa), and 1 in 2 will be heterozygous (Aa).

Traits affected by genes on the sex chromosomes are called sex-linked traits. Most sex-linked traits are X-linked, that is, they are on the X chromosome. In contrast, only a few Y-linked traits exist, largely because the Y chromosome is extremely small, with relatively few genes. An example of an X-linked trait is hemophilia, in which the ability to produce one of the clotting factors is absent. Hemophilia is a recessive allele of a gene located on the X chromosome. The possible genotypes and phenotypes are, therefore, $X^H X^H$ (normal homozygous female), $X^H X^h$ (normal heterozygous female), $X^h X^h$ (hemophiliac homozygous female), $X^H Y$ (normal male), and $X^h Y$ (hemophiliac male). Notice that a female must have both recessive genes to have hemophilia, but a male, because he has only one X chromosome, exhibits hemophilia with only one recessive allele. The Y chromosome has no hemophilia allele. If a woman who is heterozygous for hemophilia ($X^H X^h$) mates with a man who does not have hemophilia ($X^H Y$), none of their daughters will have hemophilia (half will be $X^H X^H$ and half will be $X^H X^h$), but half of their sons will have hemophilia (half will be $X^H Y$ and half will be $X^h Y$).

The expression of a dominant allele over a recessive allele is the simplest manner by which genes determine a person's phenotype. Other ways also exist for genes to influence the expression of a trait. In some cases, the dominant allele does not completely mask the recessive allele, a condition called incomplete dominance. Another type of gene expression is called co-dominance. In this case, two alleles combine to produce a phenotype without either allele being dominant or recessive. For example, a person with type AB blood has both A antigens and B antigens on the surface of the red blood cells. The antigens result from an allele that produces the A antigen and a different allele that produces the B antigen. A and B are neither dominant nor recessive in relation to each other. An allele that produces neither the A nor B antigen is called "O." The possible combinations of blood type are AB, AO (called A), BO (called B), and OO (called O).The expression of many genes in concert is required for polygenic traits. Examples are a person's height, eye and skin color, and intelligence. Polygenic traits typically have a great amount of variability. For example, many different shades of eye color and skin color exist. Because of the many genes involved, it is difficult to predict how a polygenic trait will be passed from parents to their children. Notice, however, that even though a combination of genes determines skin color, one single defective gene can eliminate skin color completely, resulting in albinism, which is inherited as a simple recessive trait.

It is estimated that humans have approximately 30,000 genes. A genomic map is a description of the DNA nucleotide sequences of the genes and their locations on the chromosomes. The mapping of the human genome was completed February 12, 2003. Knowledge of the human genome and what effects the genome has on a person's physical, mental, and behavioral abilities will revolutionize medicine and transform society in many ways. Medicine, for example, will shift its emphasis from the curative to the preventative. The potential disorders or diseases a person is likely to develop can be prevented or their severity lessened. When prevention is not possible, knowledge of the enzymes or other molecules involved in a disorder may result in new drugs and techniques that can compensate for the genetic disorder. Knowledge of the genes involved in a disorder may result in gene therapy (or genetic engineering) that repairs or replaces defective genes, resulting in curing such genetic disorders as Huntington's disease or cystic fibrosis.

Proteins are produced from the information stored in DNA in two steps called transcription and translation. To illustrate this process, consider a cook who wants a cake recipe that is in a cookbook in the reference section of the library. Because the book can't be checked out, the cook makes a handwritten copy, or transcription, of the recipe. Then, back in the kitchen, the cook uses the information in the recipe to bake a cake. The process of making a cake from the recipe is called translation, in which, for example, F-L-O-U-R is the code for ground wheat. In this analogy, DNA is the cookbook. It's too large a molecule to leave the nucleus (the cell's library) and enter the cytoplasm (the cell's kitchen) where the protein (cake) is made on structures called ribosomes (the mixing bowl). The information in the DNA necessary to make a particular protein is copied through transcription, and the copy, called messenger RNA (mRNA), goes out of the nucleus to the ribosomes. The "ingredients" for the "cake" are amino acids, which are collected by molecules called transfer RNA (tRNA) and brought to the ribosomes for assembly. Proteins may be hundreds of amino acids long. These hundreds of amino acids are derived from an "alphabet" of twenty amino acids.

Genes are stretches of DNA hundreds to thousands of letters long. DNA is made of a four-letter alphabet of small molecules called nucleotides: adenine (A), thymine (T), cytosine (C), and guanine (G). Early researchers thought that DNA, with an alphabet consisting of only four letters, was not complex enough to store all the information needed by a living cell. However, with the advent of the computer age, we now recognize that even a binary code consisting of only two letters (1 and 0) can store and transmit tremendous amounts of information. Indeed it has been computers that have permitted not only the sequencing, but also the cataloging and comparative study, of vast numbers of DNA sequences—all within the past few decades.

The DNA code is read in sets of three nucleotides; each three-letter set is called a codon. In this simple yet amazing feat, a DNA message, written in a four-letter alphabet, is used to produce a protein from a twenty-letter alphabet. For example, the three-nucleotide sequence "AGC" codes for the amino acid serine, and "GAG" codes for leucine. Some of the DNA codons provide other information. For example, the sequence, TAC, indicates the beginning of a gene, whereas ATC indicates where the gene ends. This is much like placing a capital letter at the beginning of a sentence and a period at the end.

When one gene ends, the next gene is not read until another TAC is encountered. Any nucleotides in-between are not read. The area between genes is called the noncoding area. Most of the total DNA, perhaps as much as 90%, is in these non-coding regions and does not code for proteins.

An example of the way the genetic code works is given in the following phrase: "I bought some flour. fuehns bnsdyd beteber xckfndk jdksdn snbs askksn lpsnsjk shue betyfg. Then I baked a cake." The period after "flour" ends one sentence and the "I" on "Then" begins the next sentence, no matter what is in-between. The jumble of letters between the sentences apparently conveys no meaning. (This hypothesis, though certainly accepted, is one that, as yet, we have no way of testing).

Much of the DNA in non-coding areas is repetitive. The repetitive areas are often short sequences of nucleotides that are repeated hundreds to thousands of times. The function of these regions of repeated strands of DNA is not completely understood, but it seems they either serve some regulatory function, or they may be simply "junk"—meaningless baggage accumulated along the evolutionary journey of the species—or both. Microsatellite DNA is one class of repetitive DNA frequently used in population studies. Microsatellite DNA consists of repeats of short sequences of DNA (2-5 nucleotides) repeated approximately 100 times. These repeats are scattered throughout the genome; an average human may have 30,000 microsatellite loci (a locus in this case, is the site of one repeat).

If the nucleus of a cell can be thought of as a library containing hundreds of books (the DNA), then that library contains information about the cell, including much of its structural and functional information, that will be passed on to the next generation. The books in this library also contain information about the history of the cell and about its relatedness to other cells in other people. This recorded history and genealogy has been stored in the cell's library for thousands of generations, just waiting to be read and comprehended. Today, for the first time in history, those books are being opened and read at an incredible pace.

As cells continually grow and divide, the DNA library is replicated. During the process of copying millions of nucleotides every time a cell divides, errors appear in the new sequences of nucleotides. Such errors may simply be the substitution of a single nucleotide (say, an A for a T), or the deletion of a portion of the sequence (e.g., the sequence ATACCGTT being reduced to ATAC-CG), or the duplication of a segment of DNA (e.g., the sequence ATAC becoming ATACATAC). These errors are called mutations. Enzymes in the cell with that specific function repair most of the mutations—but not all. Some errors occur within genes while others occur in non-coding DNA and are apparently inconsequential. Some mutations occur in cells of the body, which result in disease states (for example, cancer). When a mutation occurs in reproductive cells, it may be passed on to the offspring, making the offspring different in some way from the parent. As we have already seen, a mutation in a gene involved in the pathway for producing pigment can result in an albino, an offspring who does not produce skin and eye color.

Most mutations reduce survival, but some are beneficial to the organism in the face of changing conditions. For example, mutated insects can become resistant to pesticides, prompting the development of more powerful and more toxic insecticides. Mutations in bacteria may make them resistant to antibiotics. The abuse of antibiotics has precipitated the emergence of resistant bacteria, posing an international medical crisis.

Mutations that occur in the non-coding regions of DNA have little or no effect on the individual or their offspring. In other words, such mutations do not change structure or function of the individual). However, the pattern of accumulated mutations within the noncoding regions of DNA results in a relatively unique identity in the DNA of each individual and their close relatives. To illustrate, imagine yourself in a shooting gallery. There are targets and blank spaces between the targets. When a bullet hits a target, the target falls over. If the bullet misses the targets and strikes a space in-between, nothing happens to the targets. However, the pattern of hits in the space between the targets leaves a unique record of the shots fired. No two shooting galleries have back walls that are exactly alike. In the same way, mutations that "hit" genes can directly affect the individual or its offspring; but mutations in the noncoding regions between genes (targets) have no apparent effect on the individual. However, the hits in the noncoding regions (the spaces between the targets) are recorded, with no two individuals having exactly the same pattern. The pattern of hits in the noncoding regions is passed on to that individual's offspring, providing a unique record of the offspring's heritage. However, only half of the parent's chromosomes are passed to the offspring. As a result, half of the "hit" patterns are not passed from a given parent to a given child.

The discovery that DNA sequences are unique among individuals and families has led to the development of a technique for identification. This technique, called DNA fingerprinting, permits a profile of key "landmarks" to be compared between DNA samples. The procedure takes advantage of the fact that many cells are equipped with a defense mechanism to protect against invasion by foreign DNA. This defense consists of proteins, called restriction enzymes. They recognize specific short sequences of DNA, attach to those sites, and snip the invading foreign DNA strand in two. Exposing a sample of DNA to a select battery of restriction enzymes snips the strand into a collection of fragments of variable lengths. They are called restriction fragments. The resulting fragments are transferred with a pipette into wells in the gel. An electrical current causes the fragments to spread along the gel. The shorter fragments move farther than the longer ones. A researcher can label this gel with a dye, making it produce a characteristic "fingerprint" of the individual, a relatively unique banding pattern produced by the restriction fragments.

These restriction fragments from a specific locus can be compared among people or populations of people, with a specific set of fragments referred to as a restriction fragment length polymorphism (RFLP). RFLPs may change through time in a lineage because mutations either destroy existing restriction recognition sites or create new ones, thereby altering the fragment's polymorphism for that particular DNA locus. The word "polymorphism" literally means "multiple forms" and can describe restriction fragments, variations in microsatellite DNA, and genes with more than one allele commonly occurring in a population.

A group of genes or DNA polymorphisms (such as differences in microsatellite sequences or restriction fragments) linked on a single chromosome is called a haplotype. The term is a contraction of the phrase "haploid genotype." Haplotypes are commonly used in population genetics to compare individuals within and among populations. A haplogroup is a set of related haplotypes that shares the same group of alleles or DNA polymorphisms. It is usually *assumed* that the members of a haplogroup, sharing a common haplotype, form a single lineage; that is, they are all descended from a common ancestor from which the haplotype is derived. (Reader alert: See discussion of Adage No. 3 in Chapter 3.)

Most of the Y chromosome is unique in that it does not pair with another chromosome during the formation of sex cells. As a result, complications such as crossing over, which breaks up linkage groups, do not usually occur in this chromosome. Thus, haplotypes associated with the Y chromosome can be used to trace apparent male lineages for hundreds of generations. Furthermore, much of what has been said about the DNA of the nucleus (called nuclear DNA) can also be said about mitochondrial DNA (mtDNA). That is, mtDNA has genes and stretches of noncoding DNA. There are polymorphisms, such as RFLPs, which are used to identify haplotypes and haplogroups, and to infer lineages. Like the Y chromosome, mtDNA does not pair during cell division; and as a result, haplotypes in mtDNA also remain stable for hundreds of generations. Haplotypes associated with the mtDNA can, therefore, be used to trace apparent female lineages for hundreds of generations.

With this primer on the basics of individual genetics, we can now move on to the dynamics of population genetics.

Chapter Six
The Genetics of Populations

Human populations are made of numerous individuals and obviously display a wide variety of physical characteristics. This variety reflects the subtle differences (alleles) in the genes responsible for such obvious phenotypes as body physique, height, skin and eye color, hair texture, etc., and less obvious characteristics such as blood type, protein structure, and disease resistance. Population genetics is the study of the frequency of alleles in populations and the processes that influence those frequencies. Used in this sense, "population" does not refer to all members of the human species collectively but to a subgroup of individuals living within a sufficiently restricted geographical area that breeding is largely restricted to members of that group.

Like most species, human populations are rarely homogeneous in their geographical distribution. There is always some clumping or aggregation of people where resources or commerce are plentiful. This aggregation influences the flow of genes between subgroups and, therefore, throughout populations and the species as a whole. Many changes in allele frequencies occur randomly and independently between local interbreeding groups or populations. Conversely, the frequencies of genes that have ecological significance—such as those for skin color and body form, or resistance to disease—are impacted significantly by natural selection. The degree of the differences between any two groups is generally proportional to their degree of isolation or to the restriction of gene flow between them

41

and the nature of the environment in which they live. Therefore, individual populations have, to varying degrees, distinctive allele frequencies that can be used to contrast and distinguish them. Obviously, no human population is completely isolated from gene flow with neighboring populations. Indeed migration and admixture are the rule rather than the exception in human history. Hence, population distinctions are rarely clear cut; rather, they frequently grade continuously from one to the next. Often, distinctions are perceived merely as statistical differences in sampled population allele frequencies or DNA polymorphisms.

New populations are sometimes founded by a small group of individuals in which allele frequencies and/or DNA polymorphisms differ considerably from overall frequencies in the parent population, simply by chance. This is called the *founder effect*. Some alleles or polymorphisms in the original population may be completely absent in the founders; others, rare in the parental population, may have reached high frequencies in the founder population. For example, in the seventeenth century, a few hundred Dutch colonists settled in South Africa and gave rise to the Afrikaners. Porphyria variegate, a dominant disorder of blood formation, is very rare in most populations, but it occurs in about 1 in 300 Afrikaners. Most of the estimated 10,000–20,000 carriers of this disease are descendants of a single Dutch couple who arrived in 1688.

Similarly, if, because of some catastrophe, only a few individuals in a population survive to propagate, the genetic composition of the population changes dramatically as the population passes through a genetic *bottleneck*. (See Fig. 1.) The drastic reduction in the number of breeding individuals depletes the variety once present in the gene pool. Many alleles are lost and others rise to higher frequency. For example, if a given allele is present in only 1% of the population and 95 percent of that population is lost in some catastrophe (this is the actual estimated loss in Mexico's population between A.D. 1500 and 1600), the probability is only one in twenty (5 percent) that that particular allele will pass through the bottleneck and be represented in the surviving population. This bottleneck effect can be demonstrated by placing one red bean in a jar with ninety-nine white beans. Shake the jar vigorously to thoroughly mix the beans. Then, with your eyes closed, draw out five beans at random, representing the 5 percent of survivors. The chance that one of the five beans will be the red bean is one in twenty. If you repeat the experiment twenty times, on average, all five beans will be white in nineteen tries. You'll get a red bean only once.

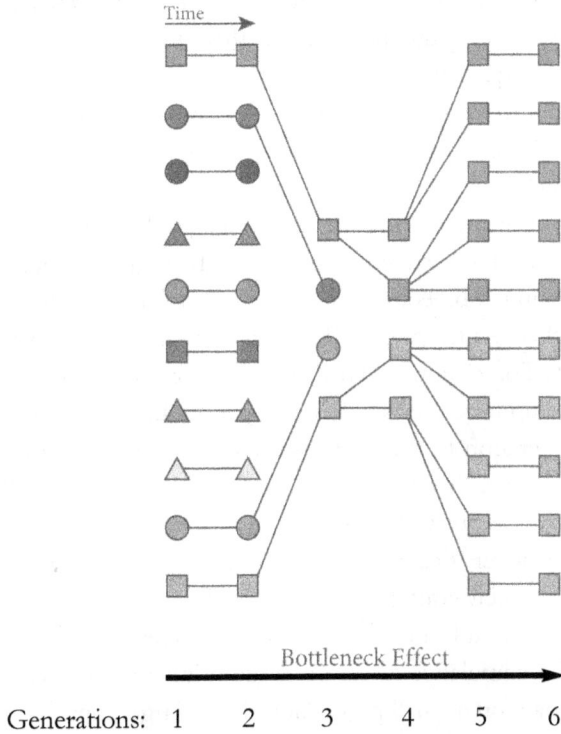

Fig. 1. A population characterized by a particular composition of allele frequencies experiences a bottleneck, resulting in a dramatically differing composition of allele frequencies.

Relatively speaking, human populations across the globe are remarkably alike genetically. Researchers see far more genetic similarity in our species than within species of our nearest neighbors, the great apes. The genetic sequences of two humans from widely separated continents are far more similar to one another than the sequences from two lowland gorillas from the same forest in West Africa. This fact has been attributed by some researchers to a past bottleneck effect in human prehistory. In contrast, other researchers have concluded that this relative genetic homogeneity is the result of rapid population growth, which tends to disperse genes uniformly throughout the population. Therefore, DNA is more homogeneous in large populations than in smaller ones. These alternate interpretations are not necessarily mutually exclusive. That is, both mechanisms, a bottleneck followed by rapid population expansion, have likely contributed to our present state of genetic homogeneity.

Population size affects the realized outcome of allele frequencies expressed in subsequent generations. In smaller populations with more limited breeding, the frequencies of alleles finding expression can change dramatically. This random sampling error is called *genetic drift*. For example, flip a penny, recording each time whether it comes up heads or tails. The up-side simulates the passing from one generation to the next of one of two variant alleles. If you flip the penny a thousand times, the resulting outcome will be remarkably close to 50:50. But if you flip the penny only a hundred times—or just ten times—the results can vary considerably from 50:50. In extremely limited runs—say, five flips—the outcome may even be 100 percent heads or, alternatively, 100 percent tails. In genetic terms, the cumulative effect of random inheritance events has a greater impact on a small population than a large population in which the averaging effect of reproduction is more spread out.

Genetic drift can also be illustrated by an example that is easy to appreciate on a scale closer to home. The sex ratio in the general population is roughly 50:50. A mother passes mtDNA is to all her offspring, but the father contributes no mtDNA. Therefore, half of her mtDNA (the half that her sons inherit) is not passed on to the next generation. Jeff and his wife have six sons and no daughters. As a result, his wife's mtDNA will become extinct when the last of their sons dies because none of her mitochondria will be passed on to their grandchildren. Instead, their grandchildren will inherit their mtDNA from the Meldrum daughters-in-law. (Of course, since Jeff's wife has sisters who have daughters, then the lineage will effectively be carried on). In contrast, if the Meldrums had only daughters, then Jeff's Y-chromosome genes would become extinct, since the Y-chromosome is passed on only to sons. But because all of their children are sons, his Y-chromosome is passed on to all six, enhancing its presence in this small population. Using just the small population of Jeff's immediate family, it is easy to see that genetic drift will explain the extinction of his wife's mtDNA and the enhancement of Jeff's Y-chromosomes genes in the population. By such means, a single mitochondrial lineage or a single Y-chromosome lineage, can ultimately spread throughout a population. Because these results are random, they are sometimes referred to as creating a "lucky" lineage. (See Fig. 2.)

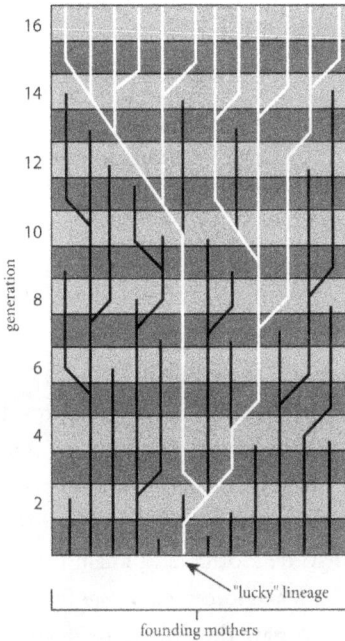

Fig. 2. Genetic drift results in a "lucky lineage" whose differential survival in the population results in a higher frequency of genetic representation.

How do these mechanisms of inheritance and principles of population genetics impact the interpretation of the genetic constitution of Native Americans? The genetic data indicate that, of the contemporary Native American populations so far sampled, the most common haplotypes are primarily similar to Asian haplotypes. However, Native Americans were decimated—or worse—as a result of European colonization. In genetic terms, these populations experienced a dramatic bottleneck in the centuries following Columbus's arrival. The Americas in 1500 had an estimated 80 million inhabitants. One hundred fifty years later, there were 10 million, reduced to 12.5 percent of the original population. In Mexico, there were 25 million natives in 1500 and one million in 1600—only 4 percent of the original population.[1] These figures are well accepted by historians and constitute the most extreme case of genocide ever recorded—an overall reduction on the order of 90 percent or more of the native population and the deaths of an estimated 70 million human beings.

How many alleles, how many mtDNA polymorphisms, and how many unique Y-chromosome polymorphisms were lost? We will never know. We can, however, state with confidence that not all the genotypes in a heterogeneous population made it through that critical bottleneck. As a result, much of the pre-Columbian diversity is simply no longer available for population geneticists to sample, and it seems unlikely that the genetic patterns of today's American Indians can be projected backward to pre-Columbian times with any degree of confidence.

The population decline in the Americas resulted from at least five causes: outright murder, slave labor in which people were essentially worked to death, the exportation of slaves, disease, and a greatly reduced birth rate.

1. Murder. Alonso de Zorita, a Spanish royal judge (1512–85), reported about 1570: "I had known an *oidor* [judge] to say . . . that if water were lacking to irrigate the Spaniards' farms, they would have to be watered with the blood of Indians."[2] Bartolomé de Las Casas, a Spanish colonist, priest, chaplain to Panfilo de Navarez (whose troops perpetrated the massacre), and first bishop of Chiapas

(1484–1566) was witness to a massacre in Caonao, Cuba, in 1519. According to his account, "The Spaniards . . . stopped to breakfast in a riverbed that was dry but for a few shallow pools. This riverbed was full of whetstones and all . . . sharpened their swords." They then reached the village of Caonao, where they decided to test the sharpness of their swords. "The whole hundred drew [their swords] . . . and began to rip open the bellies, to cut and kill—men, women, children and old folk . . . not a man of all of them there remain alive."[3] Were unique genes, chromosomes, and polymorphisms lost in Caonao? Probably, but such a hypothesis can never be tested.

A group of Dominicans reported to M. de Xeries, the minister of Charles I of Spain in 1519: "There were among the prisoners some women who had recently given birth, if the new-born babes happened to cry, they [the soldiers] seized them by the legs and hurled them against the rocks." In another account, "Some Christians encountered an Indian woman, who was carrying in her arms a child at suck. . . . They tore the child from the mother's arms and flung it still living to [their] . . . dog, which proceeded to devour it."[4] The unique genetic profiles of these lost children will never be known.

2. Slave Labor. The objective of the conquistador-colonists was to become as wealthy as possible as quickly as possible. They had little or no concern for the health or lives of the slaves who did the work or the villages from whom they demanded tribute money. Villagers sold off land and children in an attempt to pay their tribute. Whole villages were depopulated as a result. Their captors did not adequately feed the Indians who were forced to work in mines or in building cities. Many died of starvation or accidents resulting from their weakened condition. Motolinia, one of the first Franciscans to land in Mexico in 1524, stated, "It would be impossible to count the number of Indians who have, to the present day, died in these [gold] mines." Many slaves died in the reconstruction of Mexico City. According to Motolinia, "In the construction some were crushed by beams, others fell from heights; others were caught beneath buildings which were being torn down. . . . [E]specially did this happen when they tore down the principal temples of the devil. Many Indians died there."[5]

3. Exportation of Slaves. Many of the Native Americans were sold as slaves. Juan de Zumarraga, first bishop of Mexico (1527–48) described the activities of the conquistador, Nuño de Guzmán, "When he began to govern this province, it contained 25,000 Indians, subjugated and peaceful. Of these he has sold 10,000 as slaves, and the others, fearing the same fate, have abandoned their villages."[6] Those slaves who survived to reproduce would have perpetuated their genes in places such as Spain, to which they were shipped.

4. Disease. Juan Bautista Pomar, writing in 1582, stated that the Indians were more vulnerable to disease than the Spaniards due to "affliction and fatigue of their spirits because they had lost the liberty God had given them; for the Spaniards treat them worse than slaves."[7] We might also add, from a modern perspective, that their increased vulnerability was due to reduced genetic resistance to diseases to which they had been exposed. Motolinia saw the diseases plaguing the Indians as the wrath of God and a just punishment. He stated, "The first was a plague of smallpox. As the Indians did not know the remedy for the disease and were very much in the habit of bathing frequently, whether well or ill, and continued to do so even when suffering from smallpox, they died in heaps, like bedbugs. Many others died of starvation, because, as they were all taken sick at once, they could not care for each other, nor was there anyone to give them bread or anything else."[8] The Spaniards made no effort to help the suffering natives. Why fight a disease if God has sent it to punish the unbelieving?

The example of the jar of beans that we used to represent gene frequencies in a genetic bottleneck assumes that the beans were identical except for color. But if the red bean was smaller or heavier than the white beans and tended to sink when you shook the jar, the chances that you would draw a red bean would be even less than one in twenty. Likewise, if an allele in a population makes a person more susceptible to a disease, such as smallpox, that allele is even less likely to pass through the bottleneck if the disease causes the bottleneck in the first place.

5. Reduced Birth Rate. The terrible living conditions among the subjugated Native Americans also resulted in a reduced birth rate.

Juan de Zumarraga stated, "They no longer approach their wives, in order not to beget slaves. . . . Thus husbands and wives were together once every eight or ten months, and when they met they were so exhausted and depressed on both sides that they had no mind for marital intercourse, and in this way they ceased to procreate. As for the newly born, they died early because their mothers, overworked and famished, had no milk to nurse them with, and for this reason, while I was in Cuba, 7000 children died in three months. Some mothers even drowned their babies from sheer desperation, while others caused themselves to abort with certain herbs which produced still-born children."[9]

In many instances, entire tribes were driven to extinction, their genetic variation and distinction lost altogether. In 1516, Juan Díaz de Solís, a Spanish conquistador, sailed up the Uruguay River. Solís and his party disembarked on the east side of the river, the first Europeans to set foot in what is now Uruguay. Almost immediately after landing, Sol's party was attacked by Indians, known as the Charrúas. The entire landing party was killed except for one cabin boy, whom the Indians captured and kept for the next eleven years. The struggle between the Spanish settlers and the Charrúas continued over the next three hundred years. By the beginning of the nineteenth century, the Spanish had exterminated the Charrúas. Most histories of Uruguay only allude to this genocide or ignore it altogether; but one history, in a footnote, states: "The last of the Charrúas, four in number, were captured in 1832 and taken to Paris for exhibition and anthropological study."[10] Those four apparently died in Europe, never again to see their native land. Did the Charrúas possess any unique genetic markers? We will never know; and it is impossible to test any hypothesis suggesting that they might have.

In short, the population reduction and genetic bottlenecks in the Americas have forever altered the genetics of the surviving groups. The populations of Native Americas were drastically reduced by disease, warfare, and slavery. Some groups became completely extinct. Toward the end of the nineteenth century, the native population in the Americas had reached an all-time low.

Furthermore, massive population movements from Europe and Africa following the conquest of the New World created admixed populations with many of the Native Americans that remained.

Recently, scholars have expressed concern over the loss of the identity and genetic distinctiveness and diversity of ethnic and indigenous populations. The Human Genome Diversity Project (HGDP), first conceived in 1991 by Luigi Luca Cavalli-Sforza of Stanford University, has undertaken to collect samples from various population groups with the aim of documenting human genetic diversity. The initial proposal discussed three principal hurdles: sample size, comparability of methods, and admixture of populations.[11] Given more than 5,000 distinct human populations in the world, it is simply beyond the scope of any global project to study them all. A more realistic ambition, they proposed, would be sampling from 25 to 250 individuals (recommended norm 150) in several hundred selected populations. Indeed, many DNA analyses have been the target of the same criticism often mentioned for fossil analyses—small sample sizes. They acknowledged that the relatively small number of modern humans sampled, combined with the effects of natural selection over millennia, would make it foolhardy to draw definitive conclusions about human migrations.

The HGD proposal also points out that, while many studies have been carried out in the past, differences in methods make comparing results difficult. Even more fundamentally it concedes:

> Ironically, at the same time as advances in technology have made it possible to undertake a detailed study of human genome variation, the human species is moving towards increasingly intensive amalgamation. Human populations have probably always been in flux but there is widespread interest in being able to reconstruct the dynamics of human populations in the time prior to known or written history ("prehistory"), particularly in the time before the dislocations caused by the large-scale transoceanic/continental migrations of recent millennia. This leads to an interest in sampling those of the "native" or "aboriginal" populations in each region, descendants of peoples present at the time of major incursions from other conti-

nents, who seem likely to have been least affected by admixture with the incoming populations. Study of these populations optimizes the ability to reconstruct the ethnographic map to its state at the beginning of recorded history. Such ethnographically based data will improve the ability to understand the population dynamics of each region prior to this. In the absence of such sampling, the rate at which admixture and population amalgamation are taking place today is so great that in a few generations much of this valuable information about regional prehistory will be made very difficult to reconstruct.[12]

Therefore, timeliness may not be the issue at all. The assumption that "aboriginal" populations experienced negligible admixture before the intercontinental incursions by modern immigrant populations may be untenable. It is this point that has drawn sharp criticism of the HGDP. Anthropologist Jonathan Marks of Yale points out that the assumption that such populations are, and have been, isolated may be gratuitous and unsustainable. On the whole, he notes, there are very few (if any) "pure" population groups which have not intermarried as the result of migration or military conquest, drastically blurring any hoped-for picture of population genetic diversity.[13] It may not be a case of the proverbial horse already being out of the barn. Rather the horse may, essentially, never have been in the barn in the first place.

Just how isolated were American aboriginal populations? And if they weren't; what are the implications for interpreting population genetic diversity? The current state of the gene pool of Native Americans cannot be studied without taking the following factors into account: (1) the history of the population, (2) its founding, (3) the potential for repeated transoceanic infusions, (4) the natural selection experienced in novel environments, (5) and the population's decimation and exploitation through colonization, disease, and warfare. Indeed, what are the implications of these qualifying factors for interpreting those genetic data that some people suggest call into question the historicity of the Book of Mormon?

Notes

[1]Tzvetan Todorov, *The Conquest of America: The Question of the Other*, translated by Richard Howard (New York: Harper and Row, 1984), 132–42.

[2]Quoted in Todorov, *The Conquest of America*, 142.

[3]Ibid., 139.

[4]Ibid.

[5]Motolinia, quoted in ibid., 137.

[6]Juan de Zumarraga, quoted in ibid., 134.

[7]Juan Bautista Pomar, quoted in ibid., 135.

[8]Motolinia, quoted in ibid., 135–36.

[9]de Zumarraga, quoted in ibid., 134.

[10]Russell H. Fitzgibbon, *Uruguay: Portrait of a Democracy* (New Brunswick, N.J.: Rutgers University Press, 1954), 7 note 3.

[11]Human Genome Diversity Project, "Summary Document: A Report Compiled on Behalf of the Human Genome Diversity (HGD) Committee of HUGO, the executive committee for the Human Genome Diversity (HGD) Project, chaired by Dr. Luca Cavalli-Sforza, http://www.stanford.edu/group/morrinst/hgdp/summary93.html (accessed October 31, 2007).

[12]Ibid.

[13]Johnathan Marks, quoted in David King, "The Human Genome Diversity Project," *GenEthics News*, Issue 10, http://www.hgalert.org/topics/personalinfo/hgdp.htm (accessed October 31, 2007).

Chapter Seven
Native American Origins: Paradigms and Northwest Passages

One of the principal sticking points for many people concerning the historicity of the Book of Mormon has been the apparent contradiction between the prevailing scientific paradigm that *all* Native Americans immigrated to the New World from Siberia via the Bering land bridge, and the common Latter-day Saint assumption that *all* Native Americans are exclusively descendants of Lehi. The opinions appear to be much more polarized than is warranted by the scientific data on the one hand or the scriptural account on the other. The position of each side has been commonly overstated and its implications carried to unfounded extremes. We have discussed the oversimplified interpretation that all Native Americans are exclusive descendants of Lehi. In this chapter we discuss what has been concluded from the scientific evidence about the peopling of the Americas and attempt to point out some assumptions that have been made and the limitations constraining the interpretation of the data.

As early as 1589, José de Acosta, a Jesuit missionary in South America, proposed that Native Americans migrated here from Siberia thousands of years ago.[1] In 1749, George Louis Leclerc, Conte de Buffon, a leading French naturalist, proposed that Asians and American Indians shared a common origin.[2] Later in the same century, Johann F. Blumenbach, the founder of physical anthropology, proposed that the American Indians were descended from Mongols of northeast Asia and that the colonization had occurred in several waves of migration.[3]

Today, the debate among most anthropologists is not *whether* Native Americans came from Asia, but from precisely where in Asia they originated and how many successive waves were involved. Michael Crawford, an anthropologist at the University of Kansas, has conducted extensive human population genetic research in the islands of the Bering Strait. He argues that these "waves of migration" continued as late as the mid-twentieth century: "In fact the Bering Strait may not ever have been an effective barrier to human migration. . . . During particularly severe winters the sea between Alaska and Siberia freezes and the ice is sufficiently firm to sustain the weight of a human or a dog sled. Despite the most challenging political barriers and boundaries separating the USA and former USSR, there was evidence (in the form of Siberian brides on St. Lawrence Island) of mate exchanges between the Eskimos on both sides of the Bering Strait accomplished by contacts across the frozen sea."[4]

Crawford is a major contributor to work in the field of Native American origins. His excellent *The Origins of Native Americans: Evidence from Anthropological Genetics* (1998) reviews an enormous volume of research concerning those origins and is cited by several researchers in the field as the best work available of its sort. Because Crawford's review of the primary literature is so comprehensive (up to 1998) and because it is more available to general readers than the primary literature he cites, we have summarized his findings over the next few pages. Following that summary, we review the literature since 1998. We do so adding our own emphasis to his caution. He reminds his readers that the Native American population has passed through a tight, selective bottleneck and experienced a massive gene flow through hybridization from European colonization, which "has forever altered the genetics of the surviving groups, thus complicating any attempts at reconstructing the pre-Columbian genetic structure."[5] David Browman, an archaeologist at Washington University, St. Louis, in a review of

Crawford's book, agreed: "Any genetic reconstruction of the earliest migrants will necessarily be susceptible to challenge because of these two issues [bottleneck and hybridization]."[6]

In addition to Crawford's caution, we note that, while his Siberian-origin hypothesis has found the greatest support, other researchers have suggested a Mongolian origin for Native American populations.[7] Martinez-Laso et al. have pointed out that Mongolia represents a much more heterogeneous population after about 2000 B.C. than Siberia.[8]

Crawford reviewed the genetic data from human blood groups, serum proteins, red-blood-cell proteins, immunoglobulins, histocompatibility proteins, DNA polymorphisms (including mitochondrial DNA and both coding and noncoding regions of nuclear DNA), and Y-chromosome markers. Human population studies can be grouped into two types: (1) survey studies, in which genetic markers are examined in relatively large numbers of people to determine common groupings; and (2) hypothesis testing, in which genetic markers are compared between two or more populations to test proposals of common ancestry. Crawford referred to some population surveys; but his review, for the most part, addressed the hypothesis that Native Americans are descended from ancestral groups who migrated to America from Siberia. He examined data concerning three main groups: Asians (Siberians in particular), Eskimos, and Amerindians. Crawford pointed out that, by 1998, population genetic studies had been conducted for 341 different molecules in the human body. Dozens of studies of Native American populations, including hundreds of individuals, had been conducted before 1998, and dozens more have been conducted since that time with perhaps another two thousand individuals being added to the records.

Two factors make a genetic marker useful for population studies: polymorphisms at a specific locus or clusters of loci (haplotypes) that vary between populations but do not vary as greatly within a given population. In some cases, the polymorphisms were either insufficient between populations or too great within populations to be useful in human population studies. For example, phosphogluconate dehydrogenase, a red-blood-cell enzyme (protein), has turned out not to be very helpful in human population studies because its alleles are not distributed according to any clear pattern. Similarly, there is considerable variation in Rh (Rhesus) blood group (ABO) allelic frequencies in both Siberia and America. As a result, even though Rh polymorphisms are consistent with the hypothesis that Native Americans came from Siberia, the within-population variation makes the Rh blood group a weaker marker for population studies than other genetic markers.

Some other, rarer blood groups show similar patterns in Siberians and Amerindians; but again, while the pattern is consistent with the hypothesis of close Siberian-American relationships, the variation within populations is considerable. ABO blood group distributions, on the other hand, are not consistent with the hypothesis of close Siberian-Amerindian ties. Siberian populations are polymorphic at the ABO locus, with about 20 percent of Siberians having the A allele and 20 percent the B allele. About 18 percent of Eskimos also have the B allele. Among North American Indians, however, the B allele is rare, and in Central and South America, both A and B are rare. Indians in the Amazon Basin are essentially all O, with no A or B alleles in the population. Crawford proposes that the A and B alleles in South American Indians were "lost in some populations through the founder effect, genetic drift, and possibly selection."[9] We agree with Crawford's explanation, but we also recognize that such a hypothesis is not testable—and probably never will be.

Conversely, several genetic markers provide powerful tests of hypotheses concerning human populations. A rare change in a protein can be a strong indicator of common heritage, if we can reasonably assume that it resulted from a unique event rather than arising independently multiple times. For example, a rare mutation in a serum protein called transferrin is seen in the Nganasan of Siberia and also in the Blackfoot Indians of Montana, suggesting a possible common origin.[10]

Studies of phosphoglucomutase, a group of red-blood-cell enzymes (proteins) derived from three genes on chromosomes 1, 4, and 6 have revealed that most Amerindians cluster in one group while the Apache, Eskimos, and Asians form another cluster.[11]

Results from these data, compared to those previously cited, suggest that Asian-American genetic relationships are varied and complex rather than the result of a single homogeneous migration of Asians. Thus, we should avoid overgeneralizations about Asian origins of Native Americans.

The genes for the human leukocyte antigens (HLA) are much more potent markers for human genetic studies than most other proteins. They are located, as a linkage group (haplotype), at five loci, with 56 alleles, on the short arm of chromosome 6. It has been calculated that 300 million genetically different combinations can result from polymorphisms at these loci.[12] With so many combinations, the possibilities for interpopulation differences are huge, whereas, because each haplotype tends to be rather stable, the intrapopulation variation is small.

An analogy will show the power of the HLA genetic markers in population studies. Imagine taking twenty sheets of paper and marking each with some random combination of five dots. Then make one photocopy of each sheet, one of each of those sheets, one of each of those, etc., until each original has a total of a thousand successive copies. Then mix up all twenty thousand sheets and hand them to someone to sort out. During the process of photocopying, small variations may be introduced, but the basic pattern will tend to come through on all thousand copies of each original. The odds are high that the sorter, given enough patience, will end up with twenty similarity groups.

Population geneticists have done just this type of sorting with human HLA combinations. For example, in 1977, Greenacre and Degos performed just such a study in 124 samples from seventy countries.[13] The data from their study allowed them to separate Asians, Eskimos, and Amerindians from Europeans, Africans, and other populations. Crawford commented of this and similar studies: "From this analysis it is clear that, on the basis of the HLA system, New World populations can be distinguished from all other groups but Asians. Asian populations share many HLA alleles with Amerindians, reflecting their close evolutionary ties."[14]

A study published in 2001 by Martinez-Laso et al. demonstrated that, based on HLA polymorphisms, "Amerindians are grouped together, and are separated from the Orientals, Siberians, Polynesians, Micronesians, Australian Aborigines, Eskimos, and Na-Dene American Indians . . . conferring a specific HLA genetic background on Amerindians."[15] Their conclusion? Amerindians have "a different origin . . . than the Na-Dane and Eskimo Native American group. This is also supported by other genetic . . . and cultural data."[16] Although this study did not demonstrate any connection to some other non-Siberian founder population, this is just the type of unique marker data one might expect from a small, isolated group embedded within a larger population. Martinez-Laso and his colleagues proposed that "Meso and South American Indians could have come from Asia and their HLA antigenic profile could have been changed due to the severe bottleneck that they suffered with the European Invasions after 1492."[17] This is exactly the type of bottleneck effect that we have already discussed.

Just as a bottleneck can differentially preserve a specific marker, like a HLA polymorphism, it can also eliminate markers from specific founder populations, erasing evidence of their apparent contributions. Martinez-Laso et al. suggested that certain hybrid HLA genes could make Amerindians more resistant to European-borne diseases, thus allowing people with such genes to better survive the bottleneck. This research team concluded: "Thus, the problem of Amerindian origin is still open: they are probably different from all world populations. . . . However, Na-Dene North American Indians and Eskimos show an altogether different HLA profile; they are related to some Asian groups. . . . If Meso and South American Indians come from Asia, they must have originated from very different Asian people to those existing nowadays. The physical anthropology of South Americans is very different from Asians."[18]

Why is this genetic marker telling a somewhat different story from that of hundreds of studies of other genetic markers? Martinez-Laso et al. explain: "The HLA system is the most polymorphic genetic system described in humans. . . . Thus, the analysis of the HLA allelism represents a valuable tool to trace migration of ancient human populations and also the ethnical composition of the present day populations. . . . This system is a unique tool for studying the origins of relatively isolated groups."[19]

Mitochondrial DNA (mtDNA) variation provides another powerful tool in the study of human populations. mtDNA can be digested with restriction endonucleases (enzymes that chop the mtDNA into smaller pieces) yielding restriction fragments. Variations in the lengths of those fragments, called restriction fragment-length polymorphisms (RFLPs) can be compared between individuals or populations. This technique was first applied to the problem of North American Indian origins by D. C. Wallace, K. Garrison, and W. C. Knowler in 1985. They found that Southwest American Indian mtDNA exhibited "Asian" RFLPs "but at frequencies very different from those found in Asia. One rare Asian HincII RFLP was found in 40 percent of the Amerindians." They concluded that "these results suggest that Amerindian tribes were founded by small numbers of female lineages and that new mutations have been fixed in these lineages since their separation from Asia."[20]

In 1993, Antonio Torroni at Emory University and colleagues at several universities in the United States, Argentina, and Russia, examined mtDNA variation in 321 individuals from seventeen Native American populations and 411 individuals from ten aboriginal Siberian populations by means of high-resolution restriction endonuclease analysis.[21] They found that most of the nearly 200 closely related RFLP haplotypes that occurred in the two populations fell into one of four clusters of haplotype groups (haplogroups), which were designated A, B, C, and D. These four haplogroups accounted for 96.9 percent of the variation in Amerindian DNA.[22] They found all four haplogroups in the Amerindian populations but only three (A, C, and D) in the Siberian population. Although haplogroup B appears in other Asian populations, it is missing in Siberia. Furthermore, intrapopulation differences within the haplogroups suggested that, whereas Siberian and Amerindian haplogroups A and C diverged 23,000 to 48,000 years ago, haplogroup D diverged 13,000–27,000 years ago, and haplogroup B diverged within Amerindian populations or from some non-Siberian Asian population 6,000 to 12,000 years ago.[23] These data suggest that at least two and perhaps three separate emigrations occurred from Asia, at least one of which may not have been from Siberia.

Torroni and Wallace announced in 1995 that 718 of 743 (96.6 percent) Native American mtDNA RELPs studied to that date fell into one of four haplogroups: A, B, C, D. The remaining twenty-five exhibited other mtDNA variations.[24] Crawford offers three explanations for these twenty-five: (1) Mutations occurring among Native American populations, (2) European or African admixture, or (3) Additional Asian haplotypes coming into the Americas by migration.[25]

In 1991, Ward and colleagues sequenced a 360-nucleotide segment of mtDNA from sixty-three individuals belonging to the Nuu-Chah-Nulth Indian tribe on Vancouver Island. They concluded from their study that the founders of the Amerindian populations contained a considerable amount of genetic diversity.[26] In describing this study, Crawford stated: "The founders of the Amerindians were not merely a few bands of Asians following animal herds, but . . . the peopling of the New World was a demic expansion involving numerous populations."[27]

However, other researchers in the field have argued that the diversity can be interpreted as resulting from one migration followed by genetic divergence in the Americas. For example, Merriwether et al. (1995) identified north-south gradients for both A and B haplogroups in the Americas. They found that haplogroup A decreased from north to south, while haplogroup B increased along the north-south gradient. The three major linguistic groups collectively showed all four haplogroups; and strikingly, all four were found within a single group. They concluded: "This overall distribution is most parsimonious with a single wave of migration into the New World which included multiple variants of all four founding lineage types. . . . Alternatively, there could have been multiple waves of migration from a single parent population in Asia/Siberia which repeatedly reintroduced the same lineages to the

New World."[28]

Thus, Merriwether and colleagues did not support the proposal of bottlenecks in the immigrating populations, stating, "It is unlikely that multiple migrations from the same area would continuously choose the same four lineages from a subset of the lineages available in the parent population. Clearly, examination of the contemporary Asian and Siberian populations indicates that these four lineages are not the most common lineages in their populations, and certainly not the only lineages present."[29] In other words, the genetic characteristics of the New World population indicate that only a small portion of the genetic diversity of the parent population was represented in the colonizing immigrants. This *is* an example of the bottleneck effect.

An interesting and controversial issue concerning mtDNA haplogroups has arisen in the past few years, suggesting an early connection with Europeans in the Native American population. Bailliet and co-workers in 1994 proposed that as many as ten possible mtDNA founder haplotypes gave rise to Amerindian populations.[30] Four of those ten would have given rise to the four major haplogroups (A, B, C, D), whereas the other six haplotypes would exist among the 3.4 percent of the population not among the four major haplogroups. In 1996, Torroni and co-workers identified ten haplogroups (designated H, I, J, K, M, T, U, V, W, and X) among three European populations.[31] Haplogroup X was present in 4 percent of the population. Forster et al., in 1996, stated that they would call "X" the major haplogroup previously referred to as "other."[32] They proposed that this haplogroup was Siberian in origin. Brown et al. (1998), continuing work on Forster et al.'s X haplotype, confirmed that it was the same as the X haplotype in the Torroni European study. They stated, "Our analysis confirmed that haplogroup X is present in both modern Native Americans and European populations." The Brown study further demonstrated that haplogroup X was clearly of ancient origin: "Overall," they summarized, "these data exclude the possibility that the occurrence of haplogroup X in Native Americans is due to recent European admixture and, instead, provide a rigorous demonstration that this haplogroup represents an additional founding mtDNA lineage in Native Americans."[33]

The antiquity of haplogroup X in the Americas was confirmed in 2002 when Malhi and Smith identified a 1,300-year-old person discovered along the Columbia River near Vantage, Washington, as belonging to haplogroup X. (This individual should not be confused with the Kennewick man, which dates from about 9,500 years ago.) This finding "confirms the hypothesis that haplogroup X is a founding lineage."[34] The implications were interesting, to say the least: an ancient European haplogroup in Native American populations? Michael Brown et al. asked the obvious question: "Where did this haplogroup originate? Thus far, haplogroup X has not been detected in numerous Asian/Siberian populations." They added: "Haplogroup X is remarkable in that it has not been found in Asians, including Siberians, suggesting that it may have come to the Americas via Eurasian migration."[35]

Haplogroup X accounts for 3 percent of the Amerindian population studied to date. Added to the 96.6 percent accounted for by haplogroups A, B, C, and D, only 0.4 percent of Native Americans so far studied remains unaccounted for. Several other studies have examined the X haplogroup. For example, in 1999, David Smith et al. analyzed mtDNA samples from 70 Native Americans who did not belong to the four common Native American haplogroups (A, B, C, and D). Thirty-two of the seventy samples exhibited characteristics of the X haplogroup. These researchers concluded: "The wide distribution of this haplogroup throughout North America, and its prehistoric presence there, are consistent with its being a fifth founding haplogroup exhibited by about 3 percent of modern Native Americans." They also concluded: "The low frequency of haplogroups other than A, B, C, D, and X among the samples studied suggests a paucity of both recent non-Native American maternal admixture in alleged full-blood Native Americans and mutations at the restriction sites that characterize the five haplogroups as well as the absence of additional (undiscovered) founding haplogroups."[36]

As Smith and his colleagues have expressed it, most researchers believe that the origins of 99.6 percent of Native

Americans are accounted for by the five haplogroups: A, B, C, D, and X. But the possibility that one of the five founding groups had ancient European connections was exciting and controversial. Even the popular press picked up on its implications. Some Latter-day Saints hoped that it was evidence of the long-awaited link to the Middle East, ignoring the fact that the Brown et al. study proposed that haplotype X arrived in North America 20,000 to 30,000 years ago, long before the Book of Mormon period.

The controversy was largely put to rest in 2001, when Miroslava Derenko et al. found haplogroup X in south Siberia.[37] They stated, in their study's introduction, "The virtual absence of haplogroup X in eastern and northern Asia raises the possibility that some American Indian founders were of European ancestry. However," they cautioned, "it should be stressed that mtDNA-variability studies of the populations living in this major geographic area were performed on a limited number of populations. Some regions remain poorly sampled, and more extensive sampling is required. Moreover, some key markers, including those defining the X-haplogroup sequences, have not been typed for many different populations. These limitations do not allow correct definition of the phylogenetic status of mtDNA lineages."[38] In short, Derenko and co-workers went looking for evidence of haplogroup X in Asia. They found it in 3.5 percent of the Altaians, the natives of the Altai in south Siberia, but in no other Siberian populations examined. However, haplogroup X in the Altaians differed in some variants from the American Indian and the European haplogroup X, falling as an intermediate between those two groups. The Altaians also exhibit the A, B, C, and D haplogroups. Derenko et al. concluded, "Therefore, they may represent the populations which are most closely related to New World indigenous groups."[39]

Because of the way science functions—by advancing and then testing hypotheses—we scientists literally, most often, only find what we seek. Because the leading hypothesis of Native American origins states that the ancestral groups came from Siberia, Siberia is where we look for genetic markers in the Native American population. When faced with data that challenge the hypothesis, such as the existence of haplogroup X in the Native American population but not in the Siberian parent population, researchers cast the investigative net more widely to determine if these data constitute a material challenge to the hypothesis or if other data can be found to meet the challenge. Therefore, Siberia is assumed to be the place to look for any evidence of haplogroup X, not some far-off place such as the Middle East, which does not even relate to the prevailing paradigm. Once study data support the hypothesis and refute the apparent challenge, even if the data are not very strong (3.5 percent of the population exhibiting a variant of the X haplogroup markers), the hypothesis is presumed to have been corroborated, thus strengthening the paradigm.

Nuclear DNA studies, based on RFLPs (restriction fragment length polymorphisms) in the nuclear DNA, as well as studies of variable numbers of tandem repeats (VNTRs) in the microsatellite noncoding regions of DNA indicate that Siberian and New World populations tend to cluster as one group. Data from studies of nuclear DNA RELPs and VNTRs also suggest that no bottleneck effect can be seen among the original migrating populations. That is, no major nuclear DNA RELP or VNTR haplotypes existing in the Asian population were lost from the emigrating populations. In 1995, Bevilaqua and co-workers investigated haplotypes in the beta-globin gene cluster in 139 individuals from five Brazilian Indian tribes and identified eight haplotypes. They concluded: "Average heterozygosity . . . is markedly reduced among these Brazilian Indians when compared with Europeans (56 percent), but much less (8 percent) in relation to Asiatics, suggesting the absence of an important bottleneck effect in the early colonization of South America."[40] A genetic bottleneck would be expected to reduce heterozygosity genetic variability.

Y chromosome-specific polymorphisms are also powerful tools in the analysis of human populations. Data from such polymorphisms also indicate Siberian-Amerindian connections. Underhill and colleagues in 1996 found a C » T point mutation at the DYS19 microsatellite locus on the Y chromosome among Inuits of Siberia and Amerindians. They proposed that this mutation might have occurred in Siberia and come to the Americas during the Asian immigration to the New World.[41]

Crawford concluded his review of Native American-Asian genetic variation by stating, "We can conclude that the native peoples of the New World constitute a distinct entity with considerable genetic variation." Furthermore, "New World populations form distinct clusters. . . . Amerindians and Eskimos descended from several populations of Asians who crossed Beringia perhaps at different times."[42]

Numerous papers addressing issues of Amerindian origins have been published in the years since Crawford's review. Most are essentially consistent with the findings published before 1998. Several studies occurring after 1998 have tended more toward support of a one-migration hypothesis, but the debate over the nature of the migrations continues to be lively.

In 1999, Fabricio Santos et al., stated that the major Y chromosome haplotype, with the C » T transition, is present in over 90 percent of Amerindian populations, although other studies found it in only 60 percent of the populations sampled. They identified the same haplotype in central Siberian populations and concluded, "The presence of this founder Y haplotype in the Americas suggests a single major migration." However, they also acknowledge: "It is difficult to explain a single major migration with further differentiation for at least three major Native American groups."[43]

Eduardo R. Tarazona-Santos and others in 2001 analyzed the geographic distribution in 236 native South Americans of Y-chromosome polymorphisms based on a high-frequency Native American haplogroup and six Y-chromosome-linked microsatellites. They found considerable Y-chromosome genetic variability in South America with Andean populations exhibiting significantly higher levels of variability than those in the continent's eastern countries. Based on these data, they proposed a model for the evolution of male lineages of South Amerindians that involves differential patterns of genetic drift and gene flow. According to this model, populations in the western part of the continent were relatively large with a considerable amount of gene flow, which created a trend toward more variability in the gene pool. Eastern South American populations, on the other hand, exhibited higher rates of genetic drift and lower levels of gene flow, which tended to isolate small populations, resulting in less genetic diversity. Their model implies that South American populations should be considered as two groups evolving at different rates. The central Andes represent a wide area that is free of barriers to gene flow. In contrast, areas of sharp genetic discontinuities appear in the eastern part of South America as do barriers to gene flow between the western and eastern parts of South America.[44]

N. R. Mesa and colleagues in 2000 found genetic evidence in Colombian populations suggesting an asymmetric mating pattern involving mostly immigrant European men and native women.[45] D. R. Carvalho-Silva et al. obtained similar results in 2001. They examined Y-chromosome DNA polymorphisms in the present-day white Brazilian population. They examined twelve polymorphisms in 200 males from four regions of Brazil and from 93 Portuguese males. They found that the vast majority of Y-chromosomes from these white Brazilian males were, not surprisingly, of European origin. There were "distinct footprints of Italian immigration to southern Brazil, migration of Moroccan Jews to the Amazon region, and possible relics of the 17th-century Dutch invasion of northeast Brazil . . . seen in the data." Only 2.5 percent of the Y-chromosome lineages in this study were found to be from sub-Saharan Africa, and none were Amerindian. In sharp contrast, the mtDNA data from white Brazilians showed that more than 60 percent of the maternal lineages were Amerindian or African. They concluded, "Together, these results configure a picture of strong directional mating between European males and Amerindian and African females, which agree[s] with the known history of the peopling of Brazil since 1500."[46]

The next year, Lell et al. identified 15 South American haplogroups associated with the Y chromosome among 549 individuals from Siberia and the Americas. The major lineage, designated haplogroup M3, accounted for 66 percent of the Native Americans examined. A second haplogroup, M45, accounted for another 25 percent, and another 5 percent was haplogroup RPS4Y-T. All three haplogroups are also found in Siberia. Lell et al. concluded, "These data suggest that Native American male lineages were derived from two major Siberian migrations."[47]

Tarazona-Santos and Santos in 2002 critiqued Lell et al., arguing that "the first settlement of the Americas has been associated with a probable bottleneck event" and that the claim of a second major migration is not necessary to explain the haplogroup distributions described by Lell et al. Tarazona-Santos and Santos argued that the Siberian natives were characterized by genetic diversity from which the emigrating peoples drew a subset of genetic variation. They also proposed that some of the Y chromosome polymorphism that Lell et al. used to support the idea of a second migration actually came from Europeans after 1500.[48]

Barjas-Castro et al. (2003) examined O allele polymorphisms (in the ABO blood groups) among the Parakana Indians, an isolated native population in the Amazon. They found unique deletions and mutations patterns in the Parakana O alleles and concluded: "Our results are in agreement with other genetic markers studied previously in Parakana Indians, whose distinct genetic pattern differs from Europeans and even from other Amerindians."[49] B. F. Corella et al. examined mtDNA polymorphisms in the HVR-1 control region among the Movima, Yuracare, Ignaciano, and Trinitario Amerindians of the "Bolivian lowlands of the Amazonian basin [the Beni region]." They concluded: "The phylogenetic comparison revealed unique lineages in the Beni areas, not reported for other Amerindian populations."[50]

In the wake of the accumulated genetic data briefly reported here, the Asian origin paradigm has become monolithic in some scientific circles, excluding any and all suggestions of other cultural or genetic infusions and influences. Forster et al. stated in 1996, "The timing and number of prehistoric migrations involved in the settlement of the American continent are subject to intense debate."[51] This statement is true; no other issues are even mentioned. There is also a considerable body of accumulated data—archeological, linguistic, and craniodental—complementing the genetic data and therefore supporting the Asian origin paradigm. Consequently, little if any evidence seriously considered by the mainstream scientific community indicates a Middle East origin (or any other origin) for any fraction—let alone the majority—of contemporary Native Americans.

However, there is persistent evidence for multiple and diverse contacts between the Americas and the Old World. These data are unrelenting in their demands for explanation and accommodation and are undermining the prevailing monolithic paradigm of Native American origins.

In 1998, Charles Petit, award-winning science journalist, stated, "Just five years ago, nothing new was possible in American prehistory, because of dogma. Now everything is possible; the veil has been lifted."[52] He found a growing opinion inferred from new data, that now the story "is that many people migrated to the New World along the coast instead of overland." For example, Dennis Stanford, chairman of the Anthropology Department at the Smithsonian Institution, is among a growing number of scientists advancing the "still heretical" belief that the first North Americans did not walk over in one main migration, but came much earlier and by boat.[53]

Concerning the present state of knowledge, *National Geographic* writer Michael Parfit said in 2000, "Today the study of who the first Americans were ... is in turmoil. ... Ten years ago most experts would have agreed that the first Americans arrived about 14,000 years ago by walking across a land bridge connecting Siberia and Alaska. ... Some suggest that instead of a single first migration, people came in a complex series of waves. The idea that they walked across land has been challenged by theories that some came by boat."[54]

At present, more sensitive population genetic analyses, such as HLA profiles, allude to a heterogeneous origin for the first Americans. As Martinez-Laso et al. concluded from their study, "The problem of Amerindian origin is still open. ... *If* Meso and South American Indians come from Asia, they must have originated from *very different* Asian people to those existing nowadays."[55]

The simplistic paradigm that *all* Native American ancestors walked together from Siberia to America must be set aside as evidence for multiple episodes of terrestrial and oceanic emigration and diffusion accumulate.

Notes

[1]Nemecek Sasha, "Who Were the First Americans?" *Scientific American*, September 2000, 81.

[2]Conte de Buffon, quoted in Michael H. Crawford, *The Origins of Native Americans: Evidence from Anthropological Genetics* (Cambridge, Eng.: Cambridge University Press, 1998), 3.

[3]Johann F. Blumenbach, quoted in ibid., 3.

[4]Ibid., 12.

[5]Ibid.

[6]David Browman, Review of Michael H. Crawford, *The Origins of Native Americans: Evidence from Anthropological Genetics*, htpp://www.socarchsci.org/bulletin/9809/9809r.htm (accessed November 1, 2007).

[7]C. J. Kolman et al., "Mitochondrial DNA Analysis of Mongolian Populations and Implications for the Origin of New World Founders," *Genetics* 142 (1996): 1321–34; D. A. Merriwether et al., "mtDNA Variation Indicates Mongolia May Have Been the Source for the Founding Population for the New World," *American Journal of Human Genetics* 59 (1996): 204–12.

[8]J. Martinez-Laso et al., "HLA Molecular Markers in Tuvinians: A Population with Both Oriental and Caucasoid Characteristics," *Annals of Human Genetics* 65 (2001): 245–61.

[9]Crawford, *The Origins of Native Americans*, 95–98.

[10]Ibid., 111–12.

[11]Ibid., 117–18.

[12]Ibid., 128–34.

[13]M. J. Greenacre and L. Degos, "Correspondence Analysis of HLA Gene Frequency Data from 124 Population Samples," *American Journal of Human Genetics* 29 (1977): 60–75.

[14]Crawford, *The Origins of Native Americans*, 132.

[15]J. Martinez-Laso et al., "HLA Molecular Markers in Tuvinians," 252.

[16]Ibid., 256–58.

[17]Ibid., 258.

[18]Ibid.

[19]Ibid., 245.

[20]D. C. Wallace, K. Garrison, and W. C. Knowler, "Dramatic Founder Effects in Amerindian Mitochondrial DNAs," *American Journal of Physical Anthropology* 68 (1985): 149–55.

[21]A. Torroni et al., "Asian Affinities and Continental Radiation of the Four Founding Native American mtDNAs," *American Journal of Human Genetics* 53 (1993): 563–90; and A. Torroni et al., "mtDNA Variation of Aboriginal Siberians Reveals Distinct Genetic Affinities with Native Americans," *American Journal of Human Genetics* 53 (1993): 591–608.

[22]Crawford, *The Origins of Native Americans*, 136.

[23]Ibid., citing Torroni et al., "Asian Affinities and Continental Radiation," 585, and A. Torroni et al., "mtDNA Variation of Aboriginal Siberians," 605.

[24]Antonio Torroni and D. C. Wallace, (1995) "mtDNA Haplotypes in Native Americans," *American Journal of Human Genetics* 56 (1995): 1234–36.

[25]Crawford, *The Origins of Native Americans*, 137.

[26]R. H. Ward, B. S. Frazier, K. Dew, and S. Pääbo, "Extensive Mitochondrial Diversity within a Single Amerindian Tribe," *Proceedings of the National Academy of Science, USA* 88 (1991): 8720–29.

[27]Crawford, *The Origins of Native Americans*, 137–38. "Demic" means "people" and appears in words like "epidemic," meaning "upon the people."

[28]D. A. Merriwether, F. Rothhammer, and R. E. Ferrell, "Distribution of the Four Founding Lineage Haplotypes in Native Americans Suggests a Single Wave of Migration for the New World," *American Journal of Physical Anthropology* 98 (1995): 411–30.

[29]Ibid., 427.

[30]G. Bailliet et al., "Founder Mitochondrial Haplotypes in Amerindian Populations," *American Journal of Human Genetics* 55 (1994): 27–33.

[31]Antonio Torroni et al., "Classification of European mtDNA from an Analysis of Three European Populations," *Genetics* 144 (1996): 1835–50.

[32]P. Forster, R. Harding, A. Torroni, and H. Bandelt, "Origin and

Evolution of Native American mtDNA Variation: A Reappraisal," *American Journal of Human Genetics* 59 (1996): 935–45.

[33]M. D. Brown et al., "mtDNA Haplogroup X: An Ancient Link between Europe/Western Asia and North America?" *American Journal of Human Genetics* 63 (1998): 1853.

[34]R. S. Malhi and D. G. Smith, "Haplotype X Confirmed in Prehistoric North America," *American Journal of Physical Anthropology* 119 (2002): 84–86.

[35]Brown et al., "mtDNA Haplogroup X," 1857.

[36]D. G. Smith, R. S. Malhi, J. Eshleman, J. G. Lorenz, and F. A. Kaestle, "Distribution of mtDNA Haplogroup X among Native North Americans," *American Journal of Physical Anthropology* 110 (November 1999): 271–84.

[37]M. V. Derenko, T. Grzybowski, B. A. Malyarchuk, J. Czarny, D. Miscicka-Sliwka, and I. A. Zakharov, "The Presence of Mitochondrial Haplogroup X in Altaians from South Siberia," *American Journal of Human Genetics* 69 (2001): 237–41.

[38]Ibid., 238.

[39]Ibid., 240.

[40]L. R. Bevilaqua, V. S. Mattevi, G. M. Ewald, F. M. Salzano, C. E. Coimbra Jr., R. V. Santos, and M. H. Hutz, "Beta-Globin Gene Cluster Haplotype Distribution in Five Brazilian Indian Tribes," *American Journal of Physical Anthropology* 98 (1995): 395–401.

[41]D. Underhill, L. Jin, R. Zemans, P. J. Oefner, and L. L. Cavalli-Sforza, "A Pre-Columbian Y Chromosome-Specific Transition and Its Implications for Human Evolutionary History," *Proceedings of the National Academy of Science, USA* 93 (1996): 196–200.

[42]Crawford, *The Origins of Native Americans*, 147.

[43]F. R. Santos et al., "The Central Siberian Origin of Native American Y Chromosomes," *American Journal of Human Genetics* 64 (1999): 627.

[44]E. Tarazona-Santos, D. R. Carvalho-Silva, D. Pettener, D. Luiselli, G. F. De Stefano, C. M. Labarga, O. Rickards, C. Tyler-Smith, S. D. Pena, and F. R. Santos, "Genetic Differentiation in South Amerindians Is Related to Environmental and Cultural Diversity: Evidence from the Y Chromosome," *American Journal of Human Genetics* 68 (2001): 1485–96.

[45]N. R. Mesa, M. C. Mondragon, I. D. Soto, M. V. Parra, C. Duque,

D. Ortiz-Barrientos, L. F. Garcia, I. D. Velez, M. L. Bravo, J. G. Munera, G. Bedoya, M. C. Bortolini, and A. Ruiz-Linares, "Autosomal, mtDNA, and Y-Chromosome Diversity in Amerinds: Pre- and Post-Columbian Patterns of Gene Flow in South America. *American Journal of Human Genetics* 67 (2000): 1277–86.

[46]D. R. Carvalho-Silva, F. R. Santos, J. Rocha, and S. D. Pena, "The Phylogeography of Brazilian Y-chromosome Lineages," *American Journal of Human Genetics* 68 (2001): 281–86.

[47]J. T. Lell et al., "The Dual Origin and Siberian Affinities of Native American Y Chromosomes," *American Journal of Human Genetics* 70 (2002): 192–206.

[48]E. Tarazona-Santos and F. R. Santos, "The Peopling of the Americas: A Second Major Migration?" *American Journal of Human Genetics* 70 (2002): 1377–80.

[49]M. L. Barjas-Castro et al., "ABO Blood Group in Amerindians from Brazilian Amazon," *Annals of Human Biology* 30 (2003): 220–24.

[50]B. F. Corella et al., "Mitochondrial DNA Diversity in the Llanos de Moxos: Moxo, Movima and Yuracare Amerindian Populations from Bolivian Lowlands," *Annals of Human Biology* 31 (2004): 9–28.

[51]P. Forster, R. Harding, A. Torroni, and H. Bandelt, "Origin and Evolution of Native American mtDNA Variation: A Reappraisal." *American Journal of Human Genetics* 59 (1996): 935–45.

[52]Charles W. Petit, "Rediscovering America," *U.S. News and World Report*, October 12, 1998, 56–64. This article won the AAAS Science Journalism award in 2000.

[53]Dennis Stanford, quoted in ibid., 64.

[54]Michael Parfit, "Hunt for the First Americans," *National Geographic*, December 2000, 41–67.

[55]J. Martinez-Laso et al., "HLA Molecular Markers in Tuvinians," 245–61; emphasis ours.

Chapter Eight
Many Routes to America

The generally accepted route of immigration from Asia to the Americas is the Bering land bridge. However, during the time when the land bridge connecting Asia to North America was exposed, the sea level was as much as 300–400 feet below its present level. Therefore, shoreline settlements or evidence of sea-going migrations along that ancient coastline are now deeply covered by ocean. Submarine archeology is just beginning to provide novel clues about early patterns of migration. Human beings had obviously developed watercraft 40,000 years ago (at least), because they had reached Australia at that point, a feat that required migration across open stretches of ocean. This fact raises the possibility that seafarers settled along the western coastline of America considerably earlier than about 14,000 years ago—the traditional date assigned to the earliest incursion from Asia.

Traditional views have held that the oceans isolated the Americas. However, the overall evidence has not exclusively supported this conclusion. The story of the skulls, such as that of Kennewick man, for example, is not about a single invasion but a gradual accumulation of peoples. "This [pattern] would be consistent with multiple waves happening over time," says Doug Owsley, a Smithsonian anthropologist. "And you cannot at this time rule out people coming across the Atlantic. It would be a rich complicated story."[1]

European civilizations may indeed have been aware of a land to the west long before Columbus. Many stories survive from pre-

Columbian Western Europe of exotic flotsam drifting ashore on the western currents. Columbus was apparently aware of such stories, which encouraged him to sail west. Modern maps of the prevailing winds and ocean currents show that the Gulf Stream, the Azores current, and westerlies go from the Caribbean Islands up the east coast of North America and cross the Atlantic (from west to east) to Spain and the eastern Atlantic Islands. The Canary Current, North Equatorial Current, and northeast trade winds go from the eastern Atlantic islands (east to west) to the Caribbean Islands.[2]

A Portuguese ship captain named Martin Vicente told Columbus that, while sailing in the Atlantic west of Portugal, he pulled a piece of wood, which had been carved with stone tools, from the sea. Columbus's brother-in-law, Pedro Correa da Cunha, governor of Porto Santo, an island five hundred miles west of Portugal, also came across a strangely carved piece of wood and large hollow canes so thick "a single joint could hold a quart of wine." Such canes were unknown in Europe or Africa.[3]

Flotsam also included pines of unknown species, as well as the bodies of two dead men apparently washed ashore on the island of Flores, the westernmost island in the Azores. Their broad faces were not like Europeans, but more like "Chinese."[4] It is said that, after every storm, the beaches of the Azores and Madeiras are littered with washed-up specimens of the common horse bean, which grows along the Caribbean coast. One man recalled that, after a great storm in 1869, a number of bluish tree trunks with black horizontal stripes, were cast up on the beaches of São Miguel. These were identified as cuipo trees, which grow in Central America. The story was told in Galway, Ireland, of "two people clinging to some planks from a shipwreck, a man and a beautiful woman," who washed up on the Irish shore. They were said to be from China.[5]

A map by Andrea Bianco, drawn in 1448, shows a stretch of coastline 1,500 miles west of Africa—almost in the exact position of the Brazilian coastline. Where did the knowledge for this map feature originate? The Portuguese claimed contact with the New World long before Columbus.[6] The ability of easterly currents to transport seafarers across the Atlantic to the New World has been repeatedly demonstrated. In August 1940, the *Anglo-Saxon* was torpedoed 800 miles southwest by south of the Azores. Seventy days later, an eighteen-foot "jolly-boat" with two survivors landed in Eleutheva in the Bahamas.[7] Most people are familiar with Thor Heyerdahl's highly publicized demonstration that a papyrus boat could sail from Safi, Morocco, to Bridgetown, Barbados. The trip required fifty-six days.[8]

What about contacts across the Pacific Ocean? Flotsam commonly drifts onto America's western shores from the Far East. Trent remembers walking along the Oregon seashore in the early 1960s looking for Japanese glass fishing floats, which were said to occasionally wash ashore during storms. He has not yet been successful in finding one, but such floats are for sale in most gift shops along the Oregon coast. A 2007 article in the travel magazine *Destinations* encouraged: "When driving the Oregon coast, stop occasionally and get out of the car, especially if you're a beachcomber. In addition to seashells, gnarled driftwood, and agates polished by sand and surf, you might find a glass fishing float from Japan washed up on the shore."[9] So glass floats from Japan are still arriving on Oregon beaches.

If fragile glass balls can cross the Pacific, why not humans, over the past 14,000 years or so? The Kuroshiro Current also called the North Pacific Drift, flows steadily from Japan to the West Coast of North America, as does the Black Current from China. Researchers have suggested that these currents could also have transported boats to the New World. The North and South Equatorial Currents drive west from the Americas toward Indonesia, but a small equatorial counter current flows from the west, out of Indonesia toward Central America.

Betty Meggers, a research archeologist at the Smithsonian, has identified similarities between pottery found in Equador and pottery from the Jamon period in Japan. She thinks contacts may have occurred even earlier—as far back as 5,000 years ago.[10] Michael Xu, a professor of modern languages and literature at Texas Christian University, is among those who theorize that China had further contact with the Americas. While excavating Mesoamerican sites in the American Southwest and Central America, Xu discovered jade, stone, and pottery artifacts attributed to the Olmec, believed to be ancestors of the Maya. Artistic motifs on the objects bear an extraordinary resemblance to Chinese bone inscriptions from the Shang dynasty (ca. 1600–1100 B.C.). Symbols for agriculture, astronomy, rain, religion, sacrifice, sky, sun, trees, and water are nearly identical. "Moreover, they bear ideographic writing that has uncanny resemblances to glyphs from the contemporaneous Shang Dynasty." Reports Xu, "When I first brought my artifacts from the Americas to China, scholars there thought that I just had more samples of Shang writing. The similarities are that striking."[11] While there is little direct evidence at this time for regular trade or settlement, it is possible that Asians traveled to the Americas for thousands of years.

A growing body of academics is drawing attention to evidence frequently overlooked or disregarded that indicates contact with the Americas by civilizations across both the Atlantic and the Pacific. These "diffusionists" have been afforded little credence by the scientific orthodoxy; but as evidence mounts and more voices join in, the diffusionist position is receiving more attention. In 1990, John L. Sorenson, emeritus professor of anthropology at Brigham Young University, and Martin Raish, instructional librarian at BYU, published a 1200-page, two-volume work: *Pre-Columbian Contact with the Americas across the Oceans*, with a bibliography citing 5,100 works.[12] Marc Stengel says of the publication, "It is either a treasure trove or a refuse heap of pre-Columbian conundrums, depending on one's perspective."[13]

Vine Deloria Jr., an outspoken Native American activist, said, "This migration from Siberia is regarded as doctrine, but basically it is a fictional doctrine that places American Indians outside the realm of planetary human experiences." He added, "Numerous tribes do say that strange people doing this or that came through our land, visited us, and so on. Or they remember that we came across the Atlantic as refugees from some struggle. . . . The mainstream scholars just don't want to deal with all that." He challenged: "Why don't you guys just drop the blinders and get into this diffusionist stuff?"[14]

Arthur Demarest, professor of anthropology at Vanderbilt University, observed, "Within orthodox academics, there are a lot of people who simply dismiss the argument out of hand on the ground that the mechanics of overseas diffusion themselves are too difficult. But there are others—and I put myself in that group— who don't doubt there's been contact. . . . What we doubt is the transformative impact of ephemeral contact. These visitors, whoever and wherever they were, simply didn't transform the societies they found here." He spelled out the problem: "If successive waves of other visitors did reach the shores of North or South America, where is their material bequest? Where, for instance, are the wheels and keystone arches that flourished in the Old World."[15]

And, we might add, where are the genes? George Carter, an emeritus professor of geography at Texas A&M, "points to Hernando de Soto, who traipsed through the New World from 1539 to 1542. . . . Of that passage virtually no trace can be found."[16] Stephen Jett, a geographer at UC Davis, says Old World inventions such as the arch and wheel "are not [the] sine qua non of cultural exchange."[17] Douglas Fraser, an art historian at Columbia University, likewise observed: "If we judge West African culture by the absence of wheeled vehicles, the plow, the true arch, draft animals and milking, then the well-documented Islamic penetration of the western Sudan cannot have taken place."[18] David Kelley, an archaeologist at the University of Calgary, pointed out: "Neither the true arch nor the wheel [was] to be found in Egypt for more than a thousand years after Mesopotamian influences . . . although [those inventions] already had a long history in Mesopotamia." He continued: "In light of such evidence, it is surprising to find scholars . . . arguing that the absence of the true arch and the wheel in the New World proved that there had been no contacts between New World and Old World."[19]

The languages of the Native Americans are diverse and have proven difficult to systematize. A popular theory divides them into three main groups: Amerindians, Na-Denes, and Eskimo-Aleuts. Each is believed to represent a separate wave of migration into the Americas from Siberia.[20] But language groups do not appear to correlate well with genetic affinity.[21] In other words, contrary to prediction, the members of one language group are not necessarily more closely related to one another genetically than some of them are to members of another language group. Science writer Charles Petit cites Johanna Nichols, professor in the Slavic Languages Department, UC Berkeley, as saying that she "counts 143 Native American language stocks from Alaska to the tip of South America that are completely unintelligible to one another." She also "calculates [that] 60,000 years are needed for 140 languages to emerge from a single founding group. Even assuming multiple migrations of people using different languages, she figures that people first showed up in the Americas at least 35,000 years ago."[22]

Walter Neves, an archaeologist at the University of São Paulo, has taken extensive skull measurements from dozens of skulls. The oldest turned out to be a young woman whom he has named Luzia. "'The measurements show that Luzia was anything but mongoloid,' he says." This 13,500 year-old female from southeastern Brazil—the oldest skeleton discovered to date in the Americas—has a skull with greater similarity to Australoid and African populations than to the Asiatic people. According to the fossil record, Neves proposed, non-Mongolian immigrants were among the first to reach the Americas. They were replaced by Mongoloid groups that arrived in South America around 9,000 years ago. Summarizes Neves: "So it seems the New World has been a melting pot for millennia. Those famous Ice Age hunters no doubt did cross the Bering land bridge. . . . But they probably were not the first ones to do so, and they most certainly were not the only ones."[23]

An alternate logical hypothesis suggests that Luzia and her people may have crossed the 4,000-mile stretch of ocean between Australia and South America by boat. But how could the early Australians have traveled more than 8,450 miles in 9500 B.C.? A possible answer comes from cave paintings from the Kimberley, a region at the northern tip of Western Australia. Here, Grahame Walsh, an expert on Australian rock art, found the oldest painting of a boat anywhere in the world. The style of the art makes it at least 17,000 years old, but it could be up to 50,000 years old. And the crucial detail is the boat's high prow. This design, unnecessary for boats in calm, inland waters, suggests that it was used on the open ocean.[24] Archaeologists speculate that such an incredible sea voyage, from Australia to South America, would not have been undertaken knowingly but by accident. In 1996, five African fishermen, caught in a storm, washed up in their boat a few weeks later on the shores of South America. Two of the fishermen died, but three made it alive.[25]

The descendants of Luzia and her relatives may have been the Fuegians, the natives of the islands at the southernmost tip of South America, Terra del Fuego. The pre-European Fuegians, who lived stone age-style lives until this century, exhibited hybrid skull features that could have resulted from intermarriage between mongoloid and negroid peoples. A 2003 study by Jaume García-Bour et al. of the DNA from twenty-four individuals who died in Terra del Fuego 100–400 years ago linked them to an Amerindian ancestry. These researchers concluded, however, that their data also suggested an early genetic differentiation of the Fuegians from other Amerindian populations through the combined processes of a population bottleneck, isolation, migration, and genetic drift. They proposed an early genetic diversification of the Fuegians soon after their arrival at the southernmost extreme of South America.[26]

Anthropologists are beginning to recognize a discontinuity between the Paleo-Indians like Luzia and modern Native Americans. Other examples of Paleo-Indians that predate and show a distinction from contemporary Native Americans include skeletons identified as Spirit Cave (Nevada) man, Buhl (Idaho) woman, Arlington Springs (California) woman, and the highly publicized Kennewick (Washington) man. According to the *New Yorker*'s report of the Kennewick man discovery, on July 28, 1996, two college students were wading in shallow water on the Columbia River near Kennewick, Washington, when "one of them stubbed his toe on a human skull." The reporter, Douglas Preston, observed, "Kennewick Man's bones are part of a growing quantity of evidence that the earliest inhabitants of the New World may have been a Caucasoid people." He noted that the Kennewick skull and that of the Spirit Cave man were "'very different' from any historic-period Native American groups" and most closely resembled those of "the Ainu from Japan and a Medieval period Norse population. . . . Among these early skeletons, there are no close resemblances to modern Native Americans." He hypothesized that "the Caucasoid type first emerged in Western Asia or the Middle East, rather than in Europe" and quoted Dennis Stanford, chairman of the Anthropology Department at the Smithsonian Institution: "When the story is finally written, the peopling of the Americas will turn out to be far more complicated than anyone imagined. There have been a lot of people who came here, at many different times. Some stayed and some left, some made it and some didn't, some got pushed out and some did the pushing. It's the history of humankind: the tough guy gets the ground."[27]

Nineteenth-century portraits of some recent Indian tribes have depicted a range of features, some quite different from the "mongoloid" norm, typically equated with Native Americans. Thomas McKenney, U.S. superintendent of Indian trade, commissioned portraitist Charles Bird King in the 1820s to paint portraits of Native Americans from the eastern, southern, and plains states. One art critic, commenting on an exhibit of these portraits, noted that "MacIntosh, the handsome Creek," resembled "a swarthy-skinned highland chief."[28] One has but to examine varied faces depicted in sculpture and bas-reliefs throughout Central America to appreciate the implications for diverse ethnicity in native populations of the Western Hemisphere.

So, how do we reconcile the apparently overwhelming genetic evidence that over 99 percent of Native Americans came from Siberia with the growing body of evidence suggesting transoceanic contacts from multiple sources? Where are the genetic footprints of such contacts? Although cultural contacts can occur with the movement of very few people (consider Marco Polo, for example), how many people must move into a place for their genetic footprints to be found a thousand, two thousand, or twenty thousand years later? Could a single person bring samples of Shang writing from China to Central America without leaving a genetic footprint that could be found in population samples taken three thousand years later? Probably. How about a group of one hundred? How many Chinese would it take, landing on the west coast of Central America, before traces of their passing could be picked up in the blood of 200 Central American Indians in 2002?

The absence of evidence of such limited, restricted contact in the current Native American gene pool is not conclusive evidence that no such contact ever occurred. Likewise, the fact that we see no genetic trace of contact (where, indeed, none might reasonably be expected) between fewer than fifty people from the Middle East and extensive New World populations that numbered in the thousands or millions and had been established for tens of thousands of years is no evidence that no such contact ever occurred.

Crawford indirectly acknowledged this fact: "A considerable body of scientific evidence has been compiled about the origins of these [New World] populations. . . . This evidence indicates extremely strong biological and cultural affinities between New World and Asian populations and leaves no doubt that the first migrants into the Americas were Asians, possibly from Siberia." However, Crawford warned, "This evidence does not preclude the possibility of some small-scale cultural contacts between specific Amerindian societies and Asian or Oceanic seafarers."[29]

We should avoid reading too much into this concession. In 2000, Crawford was quoted in the *Salt Lake Tribune* in response to questions about the implications of DNA research for the Book of Mormon. He remarked, "I don't think there is one iota of evidence that suggests a lost tribe from Israel made it all the way to the New World. It is a great story, slain by ugly fact."[30] Jeff spoke to Crawford by telephone in July 2003 to place this isolated quotation in context. Crawford stood by his statement, but the conversation revealed some interesting insights. First, he assumed the Book of Mormon asserted that the American Indians are a lost tribe of Israel. He was obviously unfamiliar with the primary document about which he was commenting. Second, he ascribed all "scripture" to mythology and belief in it as a crutch for which he felt no personal need. He was incredulous that a first millennium B.C.

Middle Eastern colony could sail to the New World. There simply was no evidence of it. He quipped that you might as well hypothesize a colony "beamed here from Venus."

We were frustrated, but also amused, by Crawford's dogmatism, given the research summarized above that considerable diffusionist evidence warns against too hastily declaring such a journey impossible. It is interesting that Nephi's older brothers apparently had the same opinion: "Our brother is a fool, for he thinketh that he can build a ship; yea, and he thinketh that he can cross these great waters" (1 Ne. 17:17). The feat was apparently not a common one and neither, apparently, was the ship, for the Lord said to Nephi, "Thou shalt construct a ship, after the manner which I shall show thee" (1 Ne. 17:8).

Regardless of Crawford's hyperbole, a growing body of data suggests that the Western Hemisphere was less isolated than is generally presumed. No longer can the possibility of a small immigrant infusion to the Americas from a source other than the main population be dismissed off-handedly.

Notes

[1]Doug Owsley, quoted in Michael Parfit, "Hunt for the First Americans," *National Geographic*, December 2000, 64.

[2]Cathryn L. Lombardi and John V. Lombardi, with K. Lynn Stoner, *Latin American History: A Teaching Atlas* (Madison: University of Wisconsin Press, 1983), 7.

[3]William D. Phillips Jr., *Before 1492: Christopher Columbus's Formative Years* (N.p.: American Historical Association, 1992), 10.

[4]Samuel Eliot Morison, *Admiral of the Ocean Sea: A Life of Christopher Columbus* (Boston: Little, Brown, and Company, 1942), 60.

[5]Gianni Granzotto, *Christopher Columbus*, translated by Stephen Sartarelli (Garden City, N.Y.: Doubleday and Company, 1985), 37.

[6]Ernle Bradford, *Christopher Columbus* (New York: Viking Press, 1973), 54.

[7]Morison, *Admiral of the Ocean Sea*, 63.

[8]Thor Heyerdahl, *The Ra Expeditions*, translated by Patricia Crampton (New York: Doubleday, 1971); and Thor Heyerdahl, Carlo Mauri, and Georges Sourial, "The Voyage of Ra II," *National Geographic*, 139 (January 1971): 44–71.

[9]No author, "Treasure Hunt," *Destinations*, May 2007, 22.

[10]Betty J. Meggers, *Prehistoric America* (Chicago: Aldine Publishing, 1972), 35, figs. 14, 15.

[11]Michael Xu, quoted in Marc K. Stengel, "The Diffusionists Have Landed," *Atlantic Monthly*, January 2000, 36.

[12]John L. Sorenson and Martin H. Raish, *Pre-Columbian Contact with the Americas across the Oceans: An Annotated Bibliography*, 2 vols. (Provo, Utah: Research Press, 1990).

[13]Stengel, "The Diffusionists Have Landed," 43.

[14]Vine Deloria Jr., quoted in ibid., 47.

[15]Arthur Demarest, quoted in ibid.

[16]George Carter, quoted in ibid.

[17]Stephen Jett, quoted in ibid.

[18]Douglas Fraser, ibid., 47–48.

[19]David Kelley, quoted in ibid., 48.

[20]J. H. Greenberg et al., "The Settlement of America: A Comparison of the Linguistic, Dental, and Genetic Evidence," *Current Anthropology* 27 (1986): 477–97.

[21]L. Luca Cavalli-Sforza, *Genes, Peoples, and Languages* (New York: North Point Press, 2000), 136. See also M. E. Hurles, "Recent Male-Mediated Gene Flow over a Linguistic Barrier in Iber Suggested by Analysis of a Y-Chromosomal DNA Polymorphism," *American Journal of Human Genetics* 65 (1999): 1437–48; M. Belledi, "Maternal and Paternal Lineages in Albania and the Genetic Structure of Indo-European Populations," *European Journal of Human Genetics* 8 (2000): 480–86; I. Nasidze and M. Stoneking, "Mitochondrial DNA Variation and Language Replacements in the Caucasus," *Proceedings of the Royal Society of London Sciences*, Series B, 268 (2001): 1197–1206; I. Nasidze et al., "Testing Hypotheses of Language Replacement in the Caucasus: Evidence from the Y-Chromosome," *Human Genetics* 112 (2002): 255–61.

[22]Johanna Nichols, quoted in Pettit, "Rediscovering America," 62.

[23]Walter Neves quoted in Sasha Nemecek, "Who Were the First

Americans?" *Scientific American,* September 2000, 86. See also the BBC documentary, *Ancient Voices,* http://news.bbc.co.uk/1/hi/sci/tech/430944.stm, accessed November 2, 2007.

[24]*Ancient Voices.*

[25]Ibid.

[26]Jaume García-Bour et al., "Early Population Differentiation in Extinct Aborigines from Tierra del Fuego-Patagonia: Ancient mtDNA Sequences and Y-Chromosome STR Characterization," *American Journal of Physical Anthropology* 123 (2003): 361–70.

[27]Dennis Stanford, quoted in Douglas Preston, "The Lost Man," *New Yorker,* June 16, 1997, 70–81.

[28]James D. Horan, *The McKenney-Hall Gallery of American Indians* (New York: Bramhall, 1982).

[29]Michael H. Crawford, *The Origins of Native Americans: Evidence from Anthropological Genetics* (Cambridge, Eng.: Cambridge University Press, 1998), 3–4.

[30]Michael Crawford, quoted in Dan Egan, "BYU Gene Data May Shed Light on Origin of Book of Mormon's Lamanites," *Salt Lake Tribune,* November 30, 2000.

Chapter Nine
Lehi's Footprints

According to the Book of Mormon, shortly after Lehi arrived in the promised land, he made the following statement, "Wherefore, I, Lehi prophesy according to the workings of the Spirit which is in me, that there shall none come into this land save they shall be brought by the hand of the Lord" (1 Ne. 1:6). If we assume that Lehi was standing somewhere in the Western Hemisphere when he made this statement, then, at that moment, some physical evidence of his presence occurred. If we had been standing at the place where Lehi made this statement, we would have had first-hand, eyewitness evidence that he was there. Such visual evidence, however, is gone within minutes. If Lehi had left footprints where he made this prophecy, such evidence would have disappeared with the next rainstorm. But if no one had been there to see Lehi, does that mean he was never there? If his "footprints" are gone before anyone discovers them, does that mean Lehi was never there? No, the absence of such data cannot refute his existence; it can only fail to support his existence.

Whereas most people understand the latent nature of fingerprints and footprints, many people do not understand that genetic data are also latent. Within a matter of a few generations, most unique genetic information from an individual is gone. Here's an example from Trent's family history. We'll call it the Buchanan legacy. Julia Ann Buchanan was Trent's mother's mother. Her great-grandfather, John Buchanan III, came to America in 1800 from

Ramelton, Donegal, Ireland. His third great-grandfather, George Buchanan (born 1648) in Blairlusk, Scotland, was a Presbyterian Covenanter who fought against James Scott, Duke of Monmouth and contender for the English throne at the Battle of Bothwell Bridge, in the summer of 1680. After the Scottish defeat, George gave all his holdings in Scotland to his brother William and fled to Ireland. Ten generations separate Trent from this George Buchanan, Presbyterian patriot or Scottish rebel, depending on which side of the bridge you stood.

Like everyone else, Trent has 1,024 ancestor slots by the time he counts back to the tenth generation. The actual number of ancestors filling those slots is often less than 1,024 because of marriages between descendants of the same ancestor. For example, Trent is descended through two lines from his second great-grandfather (on one line and third great-grandfather on another line), Alexander Stephens. To his knowledge, however, descent from George Buchanan follows only one line. The progenitors of Alexander Stephens, from whom he descends by two lines, would each occupy two slots rather than one in the tenth generation while George Buchanan occupies only one. The size of the genome for every living human (or for any human that has ever lived), is approximately 30,000 genes, with at least two alleles for each gene. (Some genes have multiple copies in the genome.) Considering a minimum of 60,000 alleles, there are 61,440,000 allelic slots in the tenth generation, from which Trent's 60,000 alleles were randomly selected. The chance, therefore, of inheriting any single allele from George Buchanan is 60,000/61,440,000 or 1/1024. The probability of inheriting any single allele from an ancestor ten generations from Trent (Thomas Stephens) through Alexander Stephens, from whom Trent descends twice, is twice as great, or 1/512. The same probability applies to inheriting any one of George Buchanan's 44 autosomal chromosomes. Of 45,056 chromosomal slots in the tenth generation back, the probability of Trent's inheriting any one of George Buchanan's chromosomes is 44/45,056, or 1/1024.

The same probability, however, does not apply to the sex chromosomes, the X and Y-chromosomes. Trent's Y chromosome is derived from his paternal line only—coming directly from Thomas Stephens (born 1610) in England in the tenth generation. Trent's mtDNA comes from a Mrs. Vandenberg, born about 1657 in New York. Ten more generations back along the Buchanan line takes Trent to Walter, eleventh Laird of Buchanan, born in 1338. The probability of his inheriting any one allele or chromosome from Walter is 1/1,048,576. Ten more generations back brings him to Anselan Buey O'Kyan, first Laird of Buchanan, born in Ireland in A.D. 980. He came to Scotland to escape the Viking raids in Ireland, then helped Malcolm II, King of Scotland, fight against the Vikings in Scotland. (Some of the Vikings he fought against may have also been Trent's ancestors as he is descended, through several lines, from the Normans.) For his service to the king, Anselan was given, in 1016 the hand of Dennistoun, heiress to the Buchanan lands on the east bank of Loch Loman. Trent's chances of inheriting an allele or chromosome from Anselan or Dennistoun, thirty generations and a thousand years ago, is 1/10,737,417,000—which is about as much chance as he has of winning the lottery.

The Buchanan family is on neither Trent's direct paternal line nor his direct maternal line, so the chance of finding any genetic marker linking him to Anselan Buey O'Kyan is about 1 in 11 billion. The chance of finding a genetic marker linking him to Walter Buchanan is one in a million and to George Buchanan, ten generations and a little more than three hundred years ago, is one in a thousand. Those are not good odds if Trent is trying to identify genetic connections to even the most recent of these ancestors.

Do these data indicate that the Lairds of Buchanan are not Trent's ancestors? Not at all. He is a direct lineal descendent of Anselan Buey O'Kyan as much as he is from any other of his ancestors of that era. Furthermore, his genealogy can be traced back beyond Anselan Buey O'Kyan for seven more generations to Fargallus, who was born in Ireland in A.D. 680. These lines are well established and documented with dates and places. There is less than one chance in ten billion, however, that his descent from Anselan can be confirmed genetically. His paternal family line can be traced only thirteen generations back before reaching a dead end with Henry Stephens, born in England in 1497. Trent's Y chromosome, therefore, says that his ancestry is English, with no mention of his Scottish, Irish, French, or German heritage.

As already mentioned, his maternal line can be documented only to Mrs. Vandenberg, born about 1657 in New York. But for the sake of argument, let's say that her husband, Jan Hendrichse Vandenberg, married a Native American, which could very easily have happened. Trent's mitochondrial DNA would show that he descended from a Native American line, with no mention of his English, Scottish, Irish, French, or German heritage, even though Mrs. Vandenberg is only one of 1,024 ancestors in that generation.

The point should be clear. Mitochondrial DNA and Y chromosome DNA reveal just a tiny slice of family history. Only one out of four great-grandfathers is represented on the Y chromosome, and only one great-grandmother in the mtDNA. Go back just five generations and only one of fourteen forefathers is revealed. Another example of lost DNA evidence of a population can be found among the Phoenicians.[1] They were a group of seafaring traders living on the coasts of North Africa and what are now Lebanon, Syria, and Israel. They are described as Canaanites before 1200 B.C. The Greek word *phoinikes* means "red people" and refers to the valuable reddish-purple cloth that the Phoenicians sold. They also exported the cedars of Lebanon, famously mentioned in the Bible in connection with Solomon's temple. The Phoenicians exported so much papyrus from Egypt to Greece that the Greeks used the name of the Phoenician port Byblos to refer to books, giving us our word *Biblos*, from which "Bible" is derived.

The origin of the Phoenicians has been proposed as a "mysterious group known as the Sea Peoples ... [migrating] ... into Lebanon around 1200 B.C. and [mixing] . . . with the Canaanites to . . . create [the] Phoenician culture. . . . Could genetics show that modern Lebanese ... share the ... Phoenician heritage?"[2] Spencer Wells, a geneticist, and Pierre Zalloua, a scientist, examined Y-chromosome haplotypes among Lebanese men in 2004. Their conclusion was: "The people living today along the coast where the Sea

People would have interbred have very similar Y-chromosome patterns to those living inland. They are basically one people."[3] Therefore, the Phoenician impact on the Lebanese gene pool was undetectable. In an interview with Gore, Wells concluded, "Apparently they didn't interbreed much. They seem to have stuck mostly to themselves."[4]

Another explanation is that their genetic contribution has been "swamped out" in subsequent generations, which means that, if male descendants died out, no Y chromosome evidence of their existence would remain. *National Geographic* writer Rick Gore concludes, "And so—for the time being, at least—the Phoenicians remain glorious ghosts."[5] Yet even though no genetic evidence exists for a Phoenician influence in North Africa, the Phoenician cultural influence was significant.

Iceland is a wonderful natural human genetics laboratory. It provides a unique opportunity to compare genetic data to genealogical data. The human history of the island is quite well known, and genealogies have been obtained for all 280,000 living Icelanders. Helgason et al. studied mtDNA and Y chromosome polymorphisms among modern Icelanders and found that all 131,060 Icelanders born after 1972 could be traced back to two cohorts of ancestors, one born between 1742 and 1798, and the other born between 1848 and 1892. They were rather surprised at this result. They concluded that their data suggested "highly positively skewed distributions of descendants to ancestors, with the vast majority of potential ancestors contributing one or no descendants and a minority of ancestors contributing large numbers of descendants."[6] Here is an example of a genetic drift effect when there is no particular pressure on the population, from, say, foreign invasion, war, or disease. Clearly this study demonstrates that genetic markers do not tell the entire story of one's ancestry.

Another interesting issue relating to the loss of genetic evidence is the lack of correlation between genetic markers of race and physical identifiers of race. Flavia Parra et al. found that color and other racial features, such as hair texture, and the shape of the nose and lips, which supposedly identify a person as having African ancestry, did not correlate with ten population-specific alleles. Instead, their results showed "large variations and extensive overlaps among the three Color categories [white, black, and intermediate]." Indeed, "one black individual had the fourth lowest (least African) . . . score." They concluded, "Our data indicate that in Brazil, . . . color, as determined by physical evaluation is a poor predictor of genomic African ancestry." In another study, Estaban Parra and his co-researchers conducted a similar study in the United States and England. They found that "the strength of the relationship between skin color and ancestry was quite variable," leading them to emphasize "the need to be cautious when using pigmentation as a proxy of ancestry."[8] Bamshad and Olson discussed these studies relative to the U.S. population. The actual West African contribution to African Americans ranged from 20 to 100 percent, with the average being 80 percent. Furthermore, "approximately 30 percent of Americans who consider themselves 'white' have less than 90 percent European ancestry."[9]

Numerous examples illustrate the challenge of tracking a population's—and more particularly an individual's—genetic legacy. One's genetic "footprint" reveals a mere fraction of the combined genes of his or her ancestry. Likewise, one's phenotype (the expression of genes for body build, hair color, skin pigmentation, etc.) may not accurately reflect the sum of one's genetic ancestry, which has faded like footprints in the sands of time.

Notes

[1]Rick Gore, "Who Were the Phoenicians?" *National Geographic* 206 (October 2004): 26–49.

[2]Ibid., 37.

[3]Spencer Wells and Pierra Zalloua, quoted in ibid., 48.

[4]Ibid., 149.

[5]Ibid.

[6]Agnar Helgason et al., "A Populationwide Coalescent Analysis of Icelandic Matrilineal and Patrilineal Genealogies: Evidence for a Faster Evolutionary Rate of mtDNA Lineages than Y Chromosomes," *American*

Journal of Human Genetics 72 (2003): 1370–88.

[7]Flavia C. Parra et al., "Color and Genetic Ancestry in Brazilians," *Proceedings of the National Academy of Science* 100 (2003): 177–82.

[8]Esteban J. Parra et al., "Implications of Correlation between Skin Color and Genetic Ancestry for Biomedical Research," *Nature Genetics* 36 (2004): S54–60.

[9]M. J. Bamshad and S. E. Olson, "Does Race Exist?" *Scientific American*, December 2003, 78–85.

Chapter Ten

Who Are the Children of Lehi?

I am Mormon, and a pure descendant of Lehi. I have reason to bless my God and my Savior Jesus Christ, that he brought our fathers out of the land of Jerusalem . . . .

Surely he hath blessed the house of Jacob, and hath been merciful unto the seed of Joseph.

And insomuch as the children of Lehi have kept his commandments he hath blessed them and prospered them according to his word.

Yea, and surely shall he again bring a remnant of the seed of Joseph to the knowledge of the Lord their God. (3 Ne. 5:20–23)

In this passage, Mormon, who abridged the record of the Nephites, reveals two significant points. First, he announces that he is a "pure" descendent of Lehi. As was common in ancient (and not so ancient) times, Mormon is obviously citing his paternal lineage. His maternal heritage was not "a pure descendant of Lehi," as Lehi's sons, at least the older ones, married daughters of Ishmael. What is Mormon's motivation for making this distinction if the children of Lehi are the sole occupants of the Americas? Clearly Mormon's statement acknowledges that the Book of Mormon is a lineage record, concerned with one particular family line among many.

The second point places the first in the context of the bigger picture—the record keepers of the children of Lehi were most concerned with the covenant and with the restoration of the remnant of

Joseph to the knowledge of their God. John A. Tvedtnes, a linguist at Brigham Young University, in 2000 drew attention to the Old Testament parallel of this phrase "remnant of Joseph." When this favored son of Jacob revealed himself to his brothers who had come to Egypt to buy grain, Joseph said, "And God sent me before you to preserve you a posterity in the earth, and to save your lives by a great deliverance" (Gen. 45:7). Tvedtnes notes, "The Hebrew term rendered 'posterity' in this verse actually means 'remnant' and is the very same word used in the Hebrew of Amos 5:15—"It may be that the Lord God of Hosts will be gracious unto the remnant of Joseph."[1]

When Captain Moroni rallied the Nephites to repel Lamanite aggression, he invoked their ancestor, Joseph:

> Moroni said unto them: Behold, we are a remnant of the seed of Jacob; yea, we are a remnant of the seed of Joseph, whose coat was rent by his brethren into many pieces; yea, and now behold, let us remember to keep the commandments of God, or our garments shall be rent by our brethren, and we be cast into prison, or be sold, or be slain.
>
> Yea, let us preserve our liberty as a remnant of Joseph; yea, let us remember the words of Jacob, before his death, for behold, he saw that a part of the remnant of the coat of Joseph was preserved and had not decayed. And he said—Even as this remnant of garment of my son hath been preserved, so shall a remnant of the seed of my son be preserved by the hand of God, and be taken unto himself, while the remainder of the seed of Joseph shall perish, even as the remnant of his garment. (Alma 46:23–24)

Tvedtnes concludes that "a remnant of Joseph" implies or even directly conveys the idea of being sent to another land in order to be preserved.[2] The sojourn of Joseph in Egypt and then that of the host of Israel, was not made in isolation; others also occupied the land.

In Zenos's allegory of the olive tree, retold in full in the Book of Mormon, the gardener grafts in wild olive branches in an effort to preserve the root of the tame olive tree. "And it came to pass that the Lord of the vineyard looked and beheld the tree in the which the wild olive branches had been grafted; and it had sprung forth and begun to bear fruit. And he beheld that it was good; and the fruit thereof was like unto the natural fruit" (Jacob 5:17). The wild branches bore fruit although they were not genetically part of the tame tree. In this instance, the tame tree is the house of Israel and the wild branches represent the Gentiles. But the allegory also refers to the "natural" branches that were grafted into wild trees growing in the nethermost parts of the vineyard. They were not planted directly into bare soil.

What of the children of Lehi? In view of the persuasive case for the interaction with indigenous populations in the Americas and in light of the principles of population genetics and the evidence of varied transoceanic contacts (discussed above), what are the implications for the prospects of finding a trace of "Lehite" DNA in the contemporary Native American population, which would confirm the presence of a small colony of ancient Israelites in the Americas?

Scholarly reactions to the Book of Mormon are often biased by the assumption that it recounts the history of *all* the native inhabitants of the entire New World.[3] These scientists are rarely, if ever, thoroughly familiar with the primary text. As has been pointed out, their conclusions are as flawed as those arrived at by some Latter-day Saints.[4] What does the record itself suggest?

Anthropologist John L. Sorensen has examined the question of whether Lehi's colony encountered others upon their arrival in the New World. He cites a number of incidents in the Book of Mormon that clearly suggest others were present and, indeed, interacting with Lehi's party. For example, when Jacob the brother of Nephi had become elderly, "there came a man among the people of Nephi whose name was Sherem." Upon meeting Jacob, Sherem says, "I have sought much opportunity that I might speak unto you; for I have heard that thou goest about much, preaching" (Jacob 7:6). Sorenson conservatively calculates that the population of Nephi's party by this time could not have exceeded fifty men—the population of a small village. How could Sherem have not met Jacob previously? How would he have had difficulty encountering the principal teacher of the people? From where did Sherem come when he arrived among the Nephites? Where was Jacob going about to preach, other than in his own village?[5]

As another example, Alma the younger, on a missionary journey to the city of Ammonihah, asked a stranger for food. This
stranger, Amulek, gave an odd reply: "I am a Nephite" (Alma 8:20).
Sorenson asks, "Why would he say that? Wasn't it obvious? Clearly
Amulek had recognized Alma as a Nephite, either by his speech or
his appearance, or perhaps by the way he had referred to God when
he opened the conversation. But to what other social or ethnic category might Amulek have belonged? His abrupt statement makes
sense only if most of the people of the place were not Nephites
and also if Amulek's characteristics did not make it already apparent to Alma that he was a Nephite."[6]

Frequently, LDS readers assume that the key Nephites are
homogeneous. Sorenson briefly analyzes the assorted references
that suggest internal variety among the Nephites: "Nephite(s)" or
"the Nephites" occurs 339 times; (2) "people of the Nephites," 18
times; (3) "people of Nephi," 4 times; (4) "children of Nephi,"
twice; and (5) "descendants of Nephi," twice. The meaning of the
first expression is defined early in the record when Jacob says,
"Those who are friendly to Nephi, I shall call Nephites, or the people of Nephi according to the reign of kings" (Jacob 1:14). This
definition suggests that the label "Nephite" hinges on their political allegiance to the Nephite king and has less to do with their literal descent from Nephi or other males of his founding group.

The term "people of the Nephites" is perhaps even more
indicative of social and cultural variation among the Nephites. "It
connotes," comments Sorenson, "that there existed a social stratum
called 'the Nephites' while another category was 'people' who were
'of,' that is subordinate to, those 'Nephites,' even while they were
under the same central government and within the same broad society. Limhi was ready to accept such second-class status for his people the Zeniffites and assumed that the dependent category still
existed as it apparently had when his father had left Zarahemla."[7]

Sorenson concludes, "Hereafter, readers will not be justified
in saying that the record fails to mention 'others' but only that we
readers have hitherto failed to observe what is said and implied

about such people in the Book of Mormon."[8]

We obviously do not know any specifics about population growth among the descendants of Lehi's colony between 600 B.C. and A.D. 1500, but we can make some educated inferences based on known population dynamics. It has been estimated, based on a number of sources, that the world population in A.D. 1 was 300 million people. That population had grown from roughly 150 million in 3500 B.C., which in turn had grown from 10 million in 10,000 B.C. Therefore the time required to double the population between 10,000 and 3500 B.C. was roughly 1600 years, whereas the doubling time from 3500 to A.D. 1 was 3,500 years. The population of the world is believed to have experienced little or no net growth between A.D. 1 and 1000, ending that period at about 300 million people. And again, after the "Black Death" (plague) of the fourteenth century, the world population was back to about 300 million. Therefore, the time covered by the Book of Mormon coincided with a period of world history where the population generally was growing very slowly, due to constant warfare, disease, and famine— conditions from which the Nephites and Lamanites were obviously not exempt.

If the Lehite population, starting with a liberal estimate of roughly fifty people, was growing at the rate of world growth at the time (i.e., a doubling period of 1600 years), the entire population would have been about seventy people at the time of Christ's appearance in A.D. 34. The total population would still be fewer than 200 upon Columbus's arrival in the Americas. These numbers seem quite low, but bear in mind that higher growth rates would have been extraordinary compared to the world population at large. If we increased the population growth rate for Lehi's group to about 0.7 percent (that's the growth rate for the United States at the present, which most experts agree is phenomenal by ancient standards), the doubling time would be approximately 100 years. With such a rapid doubling period, beginning with a colony of fifty people, there would have been roughly 3,200 people in the population at the time of Christ and about 50,000 people at the time of the destruction of the Nephites in A.D. 421. If we assume that the great

battles that ended the Nephite civilization had little effect on the
total population (say only 1/200 were Nephites), then the population would keep growing unchecked for another thousand years,
reaching a total population of 100 million by the time Columbus
arrived. There are estimates of 80 million people in the New World
at A.D. 1500, which could have been achieved by a small founding
population like Lehi's colony, arriving in 600 B.C., *only* if it experienced phenomenal growth rates unlike those that existed anywhere
in the world prior to the modern era and only if we also assume no
wars, disease, or famine that affected population growth. But the
Book of Mormon record is a story of frequent wars and contention, fraught with disease and famine.

Recently, John Kunich, a judge advocate with a biology background, provided an in-depth discussion of Book of Mormon population sizes.[9] He similarly concluded that the numbers cited in the
death counts resulting from warfare between Nephites and Lamanites, or among the Nephites themselves, could not be accounted
for without invoking extraordinary rates of population growth. He
then explores all sorts of hypothetical but improbable explanations
for an extraordinarily accelerated growth rate, while discounting the
most obvious and most reasonable explanation—i.e., the incorporation of indigenous people into the ranks of the Nephites and
more especially the Lamanites. His reason for rejecting this possibility is based on his reading of Lehi's prophecy recorded in the
Book of Mormon itself:

> It is wisdom that this land should be kept as yet from the
> knowledge of other nations; for behold, many nations would over-
> run the land, that there would be no place for an inheritance.
>
> Wherefore, I, Lehi, have obtained a promise, that inasmuch as
> those whom the Lord God shall bring out of the land of Jerusalem
> shall keep his commandments, they shall prosper upon the face of
> this land; and they shall be kept from all other nations, that they may
> possess this land unto themselves. And if it so be that they shall keep
> his commandments they shall be blessed upon the face of this land,
> and there shall be none to molest them, nor to take away the land of

their inheritance; and they shall dwell safely forever. (2 Ne. 1:8–9)

We also read in Mosiah 25:2-3:

> Now there were not so many of the children of Nephi . . . as
> there were of the people of Zarahemla. . . .
>
> And there were not so many of the people of Nephi and of
> the people of Zarahemla as there were of the Lamanites; yea, they
> were not half so numerous.

This statement is very curious concerning the number of
Lehi's descendants. If we assume that there was a relatively even
split between the Nephites and Lamanites when Nephi took his followers out of the land where Lehi died and fled into the wilderness
to found the land/city of Nephi (2 Ne. 5:7), then where did all the
Lamanites come from? Mosiah 25:2–3 states that there were more
Mulekites than Nephites and more Lamanites than Nephites and
Mulekites combined. In other words, some 450 years after the separation, there were over twice as many Lamanites as Nephites. This
difference seems to have occurred during this period in spite of the
report by the Nephite recorders that they were being blessed of the
Lord whereas the Lamanites were constantly being killed off when-
ever they attacked the Nephites. Where did all the extra Lamanites
come from?

It appears that the Nephites were not all that aware of other
people beyond the immediate scope of their experience. Certainly
"others" rarely make it into the Nephite record. True, sometime
between 279 and 130 B.C. when Mosiah led the righteous Nephites
out of the city of Nephi into the wilderness (again) where they
stumbled on the previously unknown descendants of Mulek in the
city of Zarahemla, it seems to have been an accidental encounter, in
spite of the fact that they had been living in the promised land for
at least 300 years (Omni 1:12–14). Furthermore, the Nephites seem
to have had little knowledge of what the Lamanites were doing all
this time (Omni 1:27–30). Their primary interactions were hostile;
the Lamanites would suddenly burst out from the wilderness and
attack Nephite settlements. Were the Lamanites making contacts

with and assimilating other people of whom the Nephites were completely unaware, simply ignored, or did not explicitly mention?

Clearly, many who have read the Book of Mormon have interpreted "this land" to mean the entire Western Hemisphere—all of the Americas—and assumed that, in God's wisdom, all the Americas were isolated from other nations until the European discoveries beginning with Columbus (or a few earlier Norsemen, Australians, or Chinese). However, our modern notions of "land" and "nation" are likely much different from those of people in the first millennium B.C. When Lehi referred to the "land of their inheritance," he very likely had no concept of the entire Western Hemisphere. Indeed, the notion of a "Western Hemisphere" didn't even exist until after a period of extensive exploration, which would have been impossible for Lehi and his followers, at least by conventional means.

Omni refers to, "a certain number who went into the wilderness to . . . posses the land of their inheritance" (Omni 1:27). Zeniff and a band of followers went from Zarahemla through the wilderness and "after many days wandering" arrived at "the land of our fathers" (Mosiah 9:1–4). These passages make it clear that, to the people living at the time, the "land of their inheritance" was a specific place some distance through a "wilderness" from Zarahemla and that the term clearly does not refer to the entire Western Hemisphere. It is very unlikely that a group of people who routinely became lost in this local wilderness had any inkling of the geography beyond a few days' travel in any direction.

But Lehi goes on to predict the fate of the Lehites should they be slow to remember their God.

> But behold, when the time cometh that they shall dwindle in unbelief, after they have received so great blessings from the hand of the Lord—having a knowledge of the creation of the earth, and all men, knowing the great and marvelous works of the Lord from the creation of the world; having power given them to do all things by faith; having all the commandments from the beginning, and having been brought by his infinite goodness into this precious land of promise—behold, I say, if the day shall come that they will reject the

Holy One of Israel, the true Messiah, their Redeemer and their God, behold, the judgments of him that is just shall rest upon them.

Yea, he will bring other nations unto them, and he will give unto them power, and he will take away from them the lands of their possessions, and he will cause them to be scattered and smitten. (2 Ne. 1:10–11)

Kunich assumes, as have many commentators, that the "other nations" spoken of by Lehi, that would take possession of the lands of their inheritance, would be the Gentiles, specifically the colonizing Europeans. In support he cites passages from Nephi's vision, the teachings of Jacob, and the commentary by Mormon, which do indeed speak of the Gentiles scattering the remnant of the Lamanites. These later passages clearly refer to the Gentiles' future arrival, but Lehi's earlier, more general prophecy, about whether his descendants prosper or dwindle in the land, aren't initially fulfilled by the arrival of the Gentiles. What did the Gentiles have to do with the demise of the Nephite civilization, which had occurred in A.D. 421, almost 1100 years before Columbus? And was the fulfillment of Lehi's prediction concerning Lamanites delayed for an entire millennium? No; as Moroni laments the destruction of his people at the hands of the "Lamanites," he also notes that the Lamanites and robbers have turned upon themselves. In fact, he witnessed a virtual "world war" erupting in the Western Hemisphere:

And behold, the Lamanites have hunted my people, the Nephites, down from city to city and from place to place, even until they are no more; and great has been their fall; yea, great and marvelous is the destruction of my people, the Nephites.

And behold, it is the hand of the Lord which hath done it. And behold also, the Lamanites are at war one with another; and the whole face of this land is one continual round of murder and bloodshed; and no one knoweth the end of the war. (Morm. 8:7–8)

He observes that only Lamanites and robbers are left. They are the "others" from the Nephite perspective.

The annihilation of the Nephites was simply one episode of

the social and political disintegration that was taking place on a widespread scale in the region. "But behold . . . there was blood and carnage spread throughout all the face of the land, both on the part of the Nephites and also on the part of the Lamanites; and it was one complete revolution throughout all the face of the land" (Morm. 2:8).

Recent discoveries in Mesoamerican archeology have shed new light on the situation described by Mormon.[10] Archeologists and historians of Mesoamerica have traditionally considered the period of time spanning the Book of Mormon record to have been a golden age of peace. This academic reconstruction was at odds with Mormon's description of continual warfare, which reached a climax for the Nephites between about A.D. 330 and 421. However, the archeological paradigm began to shift as early as the 1950s when archaeologists discovered Mesoamerican monument art that depicted victory scenes of overlords treading on defeated rival warriors. Next, regional evidence of the fortification of large cities was systematically uncovered. In many instances, indication of rural populations is lacking as people moved into cities for protection from marauding armies. Numerous sites are described as having ditch and rampart construction, frequently from material scavenged from nearby structures. The collapse has been portrayed as involving severe population reduction, abandoned settlements, and fragmentation into small local factions. Sorenson asks, "Is the last ditch warfare and ethnic extermination in the Book of Mormon credible? The issue had not been addressed until very recently. The question is, was the intensity and scale of the warfare detected by archeologists ever great enough to account for the extermination of people like the Nephites? Now the answer is a clear cut yes."[11]

The Petexbatun Regional Archeological Project has carefully documented evidence of warfare and fortification in southern Yucatan between the eighth and ninth centuries A.D.[12] This time frame postdates the demise of the Nephite civilization, but the detailed study period exemplifies the pattern that prevailed. The project found that the region's population was virtually destroyed by a state of siege and fortification warfare. Within decades, only 5 to

10 percent of the original population remained. (For comparison purposes, the Nephite decline and disappearance took a little more than sixty years.) What toll did this extended period of warfare have on the population genetics of the Native Americans in this region? First thought to be a local conflict between rival sibling rulers, new data indicate that such conflicts were the beginning of much more extensive warfare that escalated throughout the region, precipitating the collapse of the Classic Maya civilization. By A.D. 810 almost all western Maya cities were abandoned or destroyed.[13] If Petexbutan was typical of this style of warfare, we might speculate that, during the preceding battles, the Nephites were not only essentially exterminated, but the aggressor Lamanites suffered extreme population reduction as well, especially in the wake of their continued warring among themselves. The vacant cities and abandoned villages are stark monuments to the extinct genotypes eliminated from the gene pool.

Considering those that may have survived, what are the chances of seeing their chromosomes represented in individuals from a population twenty generations later? We might point to the example of the nine-thousand-year-old "Cheddar Man" (named because he was found in limestone caves near Cheddar, England, in 1903). These bones date from approximately 7150 B.C.; but in 1997, DNA analysis linked him to a high school teacher, Adrian Targett, living in the same town today. The DNA match is very similar despite the 10,000 years that separate the two; only one base pair—that is, one letter of the genetic alphabet—is different out of three hundred. It took a sample of only twenty local Cheddar residents to find this close match with the DNA from Cheddar Man's molar.[14] The specific sequence from the tooth is present in an estimated mere 1 or 2 percent of the modern British population. Scientists said the odds of finding a match were not as enormous as might appear because of the relatively small number of people who lived in Britain's Stone Age—a case of founder effect at work.

In other words, the example of Cheddar Man turns the Lehite situation on its head. A small founding population of ancient Britons constituted the principal, if not the sole, inhabitants of the region. Therefore, shared genes of the relatively closely related members of this ancient population are expressed with higher frequency in the local contemporary resident population—in the case of Cheddar man a whopping 1–2 percent. In contrast, the genes present in Lehi's founding colony must have been a mere drop in the Western Hemisphere gene pool, making a trivial contribution, genetically speaking. Furthermore, this gene pool experienced a succession of extreme bottlenecks.

The Book of Mormon itself is clearly biased in its presentation of the record of the Nephites. However, to any observant reader the implicit acknowledgement of "others" is evident. The term "Lamanite" encompasses these other people who fought against the people of Nephi. The modest genetic contribution of the literal children of Lehi to the gene pool of the Western Hemisphere was sharply diminished during the extended period of warfare that annihilated the Nephites and then spread to cover the face of the land. The archeological record reveals evidence of centuries of extensive protracted warfare in a region that is now most commonly accepted as coinciding with Book of Mormon lands. The chances of detecting distinctive gene markers from the surviving children of Lehi, in today's Native American gene pool are, because of these constraints, expected to be extremely remote, if not altogether nil.

Notes

[1]John A. Tvedtnes, "The Remnant of Joseph," *FARMS Update* 20, no. 8 (2000), http://www.farms.byu.edu/publications/insightsvolume.php ?insightsid=148&volume=208number=8 (accessed October 31, 2007).

[2]Ibid.

[3]Robert Wauchope, *Lost Tribes and Sunken Continents* (Chicago: University of Chicago Press, 1962); Michael D. Coe, "Mormons and Archaeology: An Outside View," *Dialogue: A Journal of Mormon Thought* 8 (1973): 40–48.

[4]John W. Welch, "B. H. Roberts: Seeker after Truth," *Ensign*, March 1986, 60–61.

[5]John L. Sorenson, "When Lehi's Party Arrived in the Land, Did They Find Others There?" *Journal of Book of Mormon Studies* 1, no. 11 (1992): 4.

[6]Ibid., 9.

[7]Ibid., 12.

[8]Ibid., 34.

[9]John C. Kunich, "'Multiply Exceedingly': Book of Mormon Population Sizes," *Sunstone* 14 (June 1990), 27–44.

[10]John L. Sorenson, "Last Ditch Warfare in Ancient Mesoamerica Recalls the Book of Mormon," *Journal of Book of Mormon Studies* 9 (2000): 44–53.

[11]Ibid., 50.

[12]Arthur A. Demarest, "The Violent Saga of a Maya Kingdom," *National Geographic*, February 1993, 95–111; Arthur A. Demerest, *Ancient Maya: The Rise and Fall of a Rainforest Civilization* (Cambridge, Eng.: Cambridge University Press, 2005).

[13]A. R. Williams, "A New Chapter in Maya History: All-Out War, Shifting Alliances, Bloody Sacrifices," *National Geographic*, October 2002, xvi..

[14]Ibid.

[15]Nicholas Wade, "The Human Family Tree: 10 Adams and 18 Eves," *New York Times*, May 2, 2000; Larry Barham, Phillip Priestly, and Adrian Targett, *In Search of the Cheddar Man* (Stroud, Eng.: Tempus Publishing, 2000).

Chapter Eleven
A Lehite Gene Marker?
Comparing Apples to Oranges

Much of the present contention and confusion surrounding the question of Book of Mormon historicity reduces to the observation that there is no evident support in the DNA data for the Mormon beliefs linking Native Americans to ancient Israelites. This statement is apparently accurate, but it is not a scientific refutation of the historicity of the Book of Mormon. Science makes a testable prediction and then searches for observations that refute the hypothesis. The absence of evidence cannot directly refute or falsify a hypothesis, especially under circumstances and conditions that offer little assurance that we could expect the determining evidence to be present. In this case, the hypothesis is that a small population of ancient Israelites colonized a limited region in the Americas and contributed in some, almost certainly small, way to the gene pool of the indigenous population. Two fundamental issues remain: (1) Are there data that bear on the hypothesis, and (2) Is there an experimental design that would appropriately test this hypothesis?[1] Geneticist David A. McClellan, of BYU, poses these very questions and, after considering the many influences impacting the genetic trace of a small immigrant population introduced into a much larger indigenous gene pool, concluded, "It may be impossible to recover the genetic signature of Lehi."[2]

There are two critical assumptions upon which this hypothesis rests. First, it assumes the presence of a bona fide "Lehite" gene marker that could conclusively be identified in the contemporary sample of Native American populations. Second, it assumes that a source population for a Lehite gene marker could indeed be identified and sampled. What is the likelihood that these assumptions are valid? Given our preceding discussion of founder effects, bottlenecks, genetic drift, admixture, and natural selection, it seems highly unlikely that such a distinct genetic marker would be detected, let alone recognized under any circumstances, especially given the conditions described in the Book of Mormon and the limitations of current research sampling and methodology.

For the sake of discussion, let's accept for a moment that one could identify, on whatever basis, a bona fide lineal descendant of Lehi in today's Native American population—the equivalent of Adrian Targett. Let's also say that there was a Lehite gene marker, recognized and agreed upon by geneticists—the equivalent of the Cheddar Man's molar. What would we compare it to? What contemporary, modern population would we sample in our search for the original source of the Lehite gene marker? The logical test would be to turn to Lehi's original home—the land of Jerusalem. But the gene pool representing Jerusalem of 600 B.C. no longer exists as a cohesive population. The very motivation for Lehi's exodus was the impending destruction about to befall Jerusalem and the southern kingdom of Judah at the hands of the Babylonians.

The pattern had already been set with the destruction and captivity of the northern kingdom of Israel. The majority of the populace, perhaps numbering in the hundreds of thousands, was carried away and foreigners were transplanted in their stead. The Old Testament states that "in the ninth year of Hoshea [722–21 B.C.] the king of Assyria took Samaria, and carried Israel away into Assyria, and placed them in Halah and in Habor by the river of Gozan, and in the cities of the Medes." Then Sargon "brought men from Babylon, and from Cutha, and from Ava, and from Hamath, and from Sepharvaim, and placed them in the cities of Samaria instead of the children of Israel" (2 Kgs. 17:6, 24; see also 2 Kgs. 18:9–12). The foreigners thus relocated in Samaria eventually intermingled with the few remaining people of the northern kingdom, thus producing the hybrid "Samaritans."

A similar fate befell the southern kingdom of Judah roughly a century later, when the Babylonians sacked Jerusalem. "And he [Nebuchadnezzar] carried away all Jerusalem, and all the princes, and all the mighty men of valor, even ten thousand captives, and all the craftsmen and smiths: none remained, save the poorest sort of the people of the land" (2 Kgs. 24:14). The vacuum was quickly filled by transplants from the various quarters of the Babylonian empire, as well as by eager opportunists among Judah's lesser neighbors.

When Babylon eventually fell to the Persians, Cyrus made the rebuilding of Jerusalem a state initiative and urged the empire to support the effort. But only a fraction of the Jews opted to return to their homeland, accompanied by Persian artisans and craftsmen. The bulk remained to be wholly assimilated within the empire. Those who returned to Jerusalem were quick to intermingle with the surrounding nationalities that now occupied the territory as attested to by the vociferous denunciations of their priest Ezra (Ezra 9:1–2). Even the rulers of Judea at the time of Christ, the Herodians, were not Israelites, but Idumeans (Edomites).[3] The Jews that remained in Babylon eventually gained considerable social standing and favor under a subsequent king of Persia, Xerxes. Xerxes ruled more than 127 provinces running from India to Ethiopia. "And in every province, and in every city, whithersoever the king's commandment and his decree came, the Jews had joy and gladness, a feast and a good day. And many of the people of the land became Jews, for the fear of the Jews fell upon them" (Esth. 8:17). This political expediency resulted in new adherents to Judaism and therefore new genes added to the gene pool. Some of these novel genes certainly made their way back to the land of Jerusalem.

Given this history of attrition and admixture, what actually constituted a "Jew"? "Even in Lehi's time a Jew could be defined variously: progeny of Judah (generic), citizen of the Jewish state (political), and believer in the Jewish religion (covenant). Then as now, to many, Israel is a people; to others it is a place or state; and to still others it is an idea, concept, or ideal."[4] "Jew," "Israelite," and

"Hebrew" were once used almost synonymously, although currently "Hebrew" is seldom used in this way. One author, speaking of
the Babylonian siege of Jerusalem, writes: "So profound was the
change in national status that historians referring to the people who
survived the fall of Jerusalem in 586 [B.C.] drop the name Hebrew
and speak of them henceforward as Jews."[5]

Jews cannot be thought of as a race, for among them are
many races—Caucasian, Negroid, and Oriental. While their common origin is undisputed, mixed multitudes accompanied them
from Egypt, Jewish soldiers took concubines from conquered
nations, and the Jews intermarried with neighboring tribesmen. It is
clear that the original family strain has been much diluted.[6]

In the wake of the Assyrian conquest of the northern tribes,
a remnant of Ephraim and Manasseh dwelt in the land of
Jerusalem, the inheritance of Judah (2 Chr. 15:9). Lehi learns by
searching the brass plates, a record of his fathers, that he was a
descendant of Joseph, who was sold into Egypt. Alma 3:10 speci-
fies that Lehi was a descendant of Manasseh, Joseph's younger son.
Hugh Nibley comments: "Manasseh . . . was half Egyptian. His
mother was Asenath, who was of the blood of Ham, a pure
Egyptian. She had to be—her father was a priest of Heliopolis.
[Lehi] was a descendant of Manasseh, whose twin brother was
Ephraim. We claim that we are descended from him. He was also a
son of Asenath, the Egyptian woman. . . . They have the blood of
Egypt in them. . . . And they have about everything you can imag-
ine in the mixed blood of Egypt."[7]

What was the lineage of Ishmael, the head of the household
that joined Lehi's in their exodus from Jerusalem? Given the historical relationship of the namesake, Ishmael seems an unlikely
name for an Israelite—something like a Polish Jew naming his son
Adolf! The Book of Mormon as we now have it does not shed light
on Ishmael's lineage; however, Apostle Erastus Snow told a
Mormon congregation that the first 116 pages of manuscript constituting the book of Lehi identified Ishmael as a descendant of
Ephraim.[8] Ephraim and Manasseh were among the ten tribes that
were lost after the Assyrian conquest, with relatively sparse repre-

sentation in the neighborhood of Jerusalem. In short, even if we could sample the genetics of ancient Jerusalem, Lehite gene markers would be in a decided minority. Certainly, Lehi would have considerably less genetic affinity to the Jews in the modern state of present-day Israel. Finally, in A.D. 70, the remaining admixture of Jews and other nationalities in Jerusalem and surrounding Judea were driven from the Middle East by the Romans to complete the scattering of Israel.

Who are the modern Jews? Roland B. Dixon, a professor of anthropology at Harvard University, wrote in 1923, "The most important single factor in the differentiation of these Jews of the Asiatic borderland . . . was the conversion to Judaism in the eighth century of the Khazars [Turkish tribesmen]. In these Khazars . . . we may in all probability see the origin of the great masses of the east European Jews of today."[9] The 1980 *Jewish Almanac* begins with the following admission, "Strictly speaking, it is *incorrect* to call an ancient Israelite a 'Jew' or call a contemporary Jew an 'Israelite' or 'Hebrew.'"[10] Equating the population genetics of the modern state of Israel with that of the nation of Judah in 600 B.C. is untenable. Conclusions drawn from data based on such comparisons are bound to be misleading.

Anthropologist Thomas W. Murphy has suggested that we can look to other populations claiming a Jewish ancestry as models for what to look for in genetic markers for Lamanites. He cites the Cohen haplotype as an example of such a marker.[11] In the modern Jewish population are three patrilineal castes described by Neil Bradman, chairman of the Center for Genetic Anthropology, University College London, and colleagues: "The Priests (Cohanim, singular Cohen), non-Cohen members of the priestly tribe (Levites), and Israelites (non-Cohanim and non-Levites)."[12] Since one becomes a Jew through matrilineal heritage, the more general Israelite caste is quite diverse genetically. Only the Cohen modal haplotype appears more frequently than 10 percent (14 out of 119). In the priestly caste it is present in just over 50 percent (in a sample of 54). Bradman dates the origin of this distinct haplotype to between 1250 and 100 B.C. Murphy implies that this date has sig-

nificance, since it places the mutation within the historical range of
the Lehite and Mulekite migrations. But there is no recorded presence of Levitical priests with either group, so even if the nascent
Cohen haplotype were present in Jerusalem of 600 B.C., there would
be much less than a one in ten chance of its being carried by Lehi
or Ishmael or Zarahemla.

Murphy goes on to cite the tests of the claims of the
Lemba—a black, South African, Bantu-speaking population—with
oral traditions asserting Jewish ancestry. It turns out that only one
of the six sampled Lemba clans carries the Cohen haplotype in high
frequency, which is interpreted as corroboration of their claim to
Jewish ancestry.[13] But what if the particular clan with the high frequency of the Cohen haplotype had been decimated by disease, or
warfare, or natural disaster? What if only the other Lemba clans had
been sampled? What if the founding Lemba population had no
member(s) with the Cohen haplotype to begin with? If circumstances had precipitated any one of these scenarios, the Lembas'
claim would have had no DNA evidence to support their oral tradition. None of these hypotheticals is true; but DNA evidence does
support the oral tradition in this case, underscoring that the existence of the Lemba does not preclude other scenarios that would
be equally true. Murphy suggests: "If the Book of Mormon's
Jewish migration account were literally true, one might find similar
evidence in one or more Native American populations. But such
evidence has not been forthcoming."[14] Of course it hasn't been
forthcoming as compared to the unusual and singular example of
the Lembas. In contrast, many other claimants of "Jewish" or
Israelitish" origin have produced no genetic evidence to corroborate their claims, nor might we reasonably or necessarily expect
them to. The factors described above decrease the probability of
finding such genetic evidence, but their absence can't be used to
prove a negative.

As previously pointed out, the "Israelite" (non-Cohen and
non-Levitical) caste of modern Jews is extremely diverse. The
Cohen modal haplotype is the only potential signature haplotype
indicating Judaic origin suggested to date, and it is only present in

about 10 percent of the modern "Israelite," or more accurately designated, Jewish caste. Lehi's small colony had no Levitical priests. The people of Zarahemla ("Mulekites") seemed very eager to acknowledge Mosiah's kingship, even though Mosiah has no apparent claim to priestly authority. There is no reason to expect that a Cohen-like marker would be manifest among the Nephites, nor is the proposed comparison to modern Jewish populations reasonable. It's like comparing apples to oranges.

The real lesson from the case of the Lemba is that a population of people now acknowledged to have been historically derived from a Jewish population, has assumed the physical appearance and material culture of the surrounding indigenous people to such an extent that their claim of Jewish ancestry went unaccepted until a singular genetic trait was identified in a fraction of its population. In like manner, to what extent might the physical traits (and underlying genetic traits) of the children of Lehi come to resemble the more numerous indigenous Native Americans through admixture and cultural assimilation?

There is yet another facet to this issue of comparison. The hypothetical question could also be posed: To what extent have the very markers associated with *pre-captivity* Judah been disseminated within the Asian populations? Would they be recognized as Israelitish or even Jewish? Spencer Palmer, a professor of history and religion, published an article in the *Ensign*, "Israel in Asia," that documents the dispersion of Israelitish emigrants from India to Japan.[15] The Bene Israel ("Sons of Israel") live primarily in Bombay, Calcutta, Old Delhi, and Ahmadabad on the Indian subcontinent. They claim to be descended from Jews who escaped persecution in Galilee in the second century B.C. The Bene Israel also resemble the local non-Jewish Maratha people in appearance and customs, which indicates intermarriage between Jews and Indians. The Bene Israel, however, maintained some distinctive Jewish practices: Mosaic dietary laws, circumcision, and Sabbath observance. They say their ancestors were oil pressers in Galilee and that they are descended from survivors of a shipwreck. In the eighteenth century they were "discovered" by traders from Baghdad. At that time, the Bene Israel were practicing just a few outward forms of Judaism (which is how they were recognized) but had no scholars of their own and therefore would not likely have a Cohen genetic marker.[16]

Turning further to the east—"Behold, these shall come from far: and, lo, these from the north and from the west; and these from the land of Sinim" (Isa. 49:12). This prophecy, spoken by Isaiah, promised the return of lost Israelites from all corners of the earth, including the land of Sinim. Interestingly, "Sinim" is the Hebrew word for China. In fortlike villages in the high mountain ranges on the Chinese-Tibetan border live the Chiang-Min of West Szechuan. Donald Leslie claims that the Chiang-Min are descendants of the ancient Israelites who arrived in China several hundred years before the time of Christ.[17]

A second group of Jews in China, those of Kaifeng, some historians believe, arrived in A.D. 1127 from India or Persia. Reportedly the Persian Jews who ventured into China did not bring women for safety reasons and married Chinese women. Some wives converted—others didn't. The Chinese Jews had some subtle distinctions of physical features, but they had become nearly completely assimilated—both culturally and biologically. Contrary to the historians' reconstruction, the Kaifeng Jews claim that their ancestors came to China much earlier and are descendants of the lost tribes of Israel, not Persian or Indian.[18]

Even further to the East, one encounters some striking parallels between some Hebrew and Japanese vocabulary. For example: *Daber* (Hebrew, "to speak") seems to be cognate to *daberu* (Japanese, "chatting"); *goi* (a non-Hebrew or foreigner), and *gaijin* (prefix meaning "a foreigner" or "non-Japanese"); *kor* (Hebrew, "cold") and *koru* (Japanese, "to freeze"); *Knesset* (Hebrew, "parliament") and *kensei* (Japanese, "constitutional government"). According to Simcha Shtull-Trauring, thousands of words and names of places have no real etymological meaning in Japanese but correspond with Hebrew words. The Japanese Shinto temple strongly recalls the ancient Israelite temple, which housed a holy of holies and several gates. Several artifacts in Japan have been traced to Assyrian and Jewish sources, among them, a well in Koryugi with the words "well of Israel" inscribed on its side. It has also been suggested that the carts of Otsu and Kyoto are of ancient biblical origin, as they are different from any others in Japan. Might the ancient Israelites and their wives and children have been conveyed to Japan in these carts? Among the Samurai is a tradition that their ancestors came to Japan from western Asia around 660 B.C. "Samurai" recalls "Samaria." Some claim that the Mikado, the Japanese emperor, is a descendant of the Hebrew tribe of Gad. "Mikado" resembles "Malchuto," Hebrew for "his majesty the king."[19]

These oral traditions and suggestive archeological artifacts require further research, but they reiterate the general point that movements of human populations have been extensive and complex. Movements of small groups of emigrants and frequent admixture with newly contacted populations can have profound impact on gene pools. What are the implications of these examples of gene flow between ancient Israelites and populations in eastern Asia for conclusions drawn about comparisons between Native American populations and East Asia populations? The possibility exists, it could be argued, that the populations of East Asia are a more reasonable place to look for ancient Israelite gene markers than among present-day Jewish populations in the Middle East. We do not advocate that the overall genetic similarity between Native Americans and East Asians can be attributed to common Israelitish ancestry. However, comparisons must be made carefully while acknowledging not only the limitations of feasible tests of hypotheses but also allowing for alternative interpretations of the data.

We do think it highly unlikely that a potential, hypothetical Lehite gene marker is present or could even be identified within the modern Native American population. Furthermore, we cannot identify any existing population as representative of the gene pool of pre-captivity Jerusalem, from which the Lehites originated to serve, as a standard of comparison for any such marker. Thus, any comparison between modern Native Americans and modern Middle Eastern populations would be like comparing apples to oranges. Current circumstances make it virtually impossible to design a scientific experiment that could test the hypothesis.

Notes

[1]David A. McClellan, "Detecting Lehi's Genetic Signature: Possible, Probable, or Not?" *FARMS Review* 15 (2003): 89.

[2]D. J. Meldrum and T. D. Stephens, "Who Are the Children of Lehi?" *Journal of Book of Mormon Studies* 12 (2003): 44.

[3]William Smith, *Smith's Bible Dictionary* (Old Tappan, N.J.: Fleming H. Revell Company), *s.v.* "Idumean."

[4]E. LV Richardson, "What Is a Jew?" *Ensign*, May 1972, 14.

[5]John B. Noss, *Man's Religions*, 3rd ed. (New York: Macmillan, 1963), 536.

[6]Richardson, "What Is a Jew?" 15–16.

[7]Hugh Nibley, *Teachings of the Book of Mormon—Semester 1: Transcripts of Lectures Presented to an Honors Book of Mormon Class at Brigham Young University, 1988–1990* (Provo, Utah: Foundation for Ancient Research and Mormon Studies, 1993), Lecture 47, p. 309.

[8]Erastus Snow, May 6, 1882, *Journal of Discourses*, 26 vols. (Liverpool and London: Latter-day Saints' Book Depot, 1854–86), 23:184–85.

[9]Roland B. Dixon, *The Racial History of Man* (New York: Charles Schribner's Sons, 1923).

[10]Carl Rheins and Richard Siegel, *Jewish Almanac* (New York: Bantam Books, 1980), 3.

[11]Thomas W. Murphy, Lamanite Genesis, Genealogy, and Genetics. http://mormonscrioturestudies.com/bomor/twm/lamgen.asp (accessed November 1, 2007). An updated revision of this manuscript appeared in *American Apocrypha: Essays on the Book of Mormon*, edited by Dan Vogel and Brent Lee Metcalfe (Salt Lake City: Signature Books, 2002). Here on p. 61, Murphy shifts the proposition to statements attributed to Bradman and Profiitt by journalist Susan Mazur in "The Front Line: Mormons in the Olympic Spotlight: Polygamy and Scripture Threaten to Steal Some of the Thunder from the Winter Games in Utah," *Financial Times*, February 9, 2002, http://globalarchive.ft.com (accessed November 1, 2007).

[12]Neil Bradman, M. Thomas, and D. Goldstein, "The Genetic Origins of the Old Testament Priests," in *America Past, America Present: Genes and Languages in the Americas and Beyond*, edited by C. Renfrew (Oxford, Eng.: McDonald Institute for Archeological Research, 2000), 31–44.

[13]Mark G. Thomas et al., "Y Chromosomes Traveling South: The Cohen Modal Haplotype and the Origins of the Lemba, the Black Jews of Southern Africa," *American Journal of Human Genetics* 66 (2000): 674–86.

[14]Murphy, "Lamanite Genesis, Genealogy, and Genetics."

[15]Spencer J. Palmer, "Israel in Asia," *Ensign*, January 1971, 70–75.

[16]Shirley Berry Isenberg, *India's Bene Israel: A Comprehensive Inquiry and Sourcebook* (Berkeley, Calif.: Judah L. Magnus Museum, 1988).

[17]Donald Leslie, The Survival of the Chinese Jews: The Jewish Community of Kiafeng (Leiden, The Netherlands: Brill, 1972).

[18]Xu Xin, *The Jews of Kiafeng, China: History, Culture, and Religion* (Hoboken, N.J.: KTAV Publishing House, 2003).

[19]Simcha Shtull-Trauring, ed., *Letters from Beyond the Sambatyon: The Myth of the Ten Lost Tribes* (New York: Maxima New Media, 1997).

Chapter Twelve
Memes: Units of Cultural Transmission

King Benjamin, in the Book of Mormon, spoke to his people: "And now because of the covenant which ye have made ye shall be called the children of Christ, his sons and his daughters; for behold this day he hath spiritually begotten you; for ye say that your hearts are changed through faith on his name; therefore ye are born of him and have become his sons and his daughters" (Mosiah 5:7). This was not a genealogical relationship based on lineage or inheritance of DNA. It describes a spiritual rebirth of the individual into the family of Christ. In other words, lineage is not the only mechanism by which God's purposes on earth are to be accomplished, or his blessings realized.

Lineage and genetics are a consequence of the means by which the human family fulfills its divine charge to multiply and replenish the earth. Genetics has tremendous influence on both the individual and on the course of history, but it does not dictate one's potential in realizing the things of eternity. Nongenetic factors also exert tremendous influence on people's lives. "What, after all, is so special about genes?" asked Richard Dawkins in *The Selfish Gene*.

The answer is that they are replicators. The laws of physics are supposed to be true all over the accessible universe. Are there any principles of biology that are likely to have similar universal validity? . . . Obviously I do not know but, if I had to bet, I would put my money on one fundamental principle. This is the law that life evolves by the differential survival of replicating entities. The gene, the DNA molecule, happens to be the replicating entity that prevails on our planet. There may be others. . . .

I think that a new kind of replicator has recently emerged on this very planet. It is staring us in the face. It is still in its infancy, still drifting clumsily about in its primeval soup. . . . The new soup is the soup of human culture. We need a name for the new replicator, a noun that conveys the idea of a unit of cultural transmission, or a unit of imitation. "Mimeme" comes from a suitable Greek root, but I want a monosyllable that sounds a bit like "gene." I hope my classicist friends will forgive me if I abbreviate mimeme to meme. If it is any consolation, it could alternatively be thought of as being related to "memory," or to the French word *même*. It should be pronounced to rhyme with "cream." . . . Examples of memes are tunes, ideas, catch-phrases, clothes fashions, and ways of making pots or of building arches.[1]

Many scholars apparently, skipped right over this novel idea, without paying it much notice at all; but twenty years later, psychologist Susan Blackmore sat up and took note. In October 1998, she wrote in the preface to her book, *The Meme Machine*:

I had read Dawkin's *The Selfish Gene* many years before but, I suppose, had dismissed the idea of memes as nothing more than a bit of fun. Suddenly I realized that here was a powerful idea, capable of transforming our understanding of the human mind—and I hadn't even noticed it. . . . When you imitate someone else, something is passed on. This "something" can be passed on again, and again, and so take on a life of its own. We might call this thing an idea, an instruction, a behavior, a piece of information . . . but if we are going to study it we shall need to give it a name. Fortunately, there is a name. It is the "meme."[2]

Trent's wife, Kathleen, is adopted. She has two older brothers who are her full genetic siblings. Each was adopted by their parents (the Browns) right after they were born. The Browns were incapable of having children. Their obstetrician/gynecologist worked with an adoption agency to arrange for them to adopt a child.

Arrangements were made with a woman who was expecting and who wanted to have the baby adopted. Everything was worked out before the baby was born, and the Browns took their baby boy home from the hospital. About a year later, the Brown's obstetrician/gynecologist called to say that the same two people who were the genetic parents of their little boy were expecting another child. Did they want to adopt it? Yes, if it was a girl. It wasn't, but it no longer mattered. The happy parents took the baby boy home to grow up with his older brother. About a year later, the circumstance was repeated. The Browns had planned to adopt only two children; but when they learned that the same couple was having another baby, they didn't even qualify their answer: "Yes, we'll take it." They brought the future Kathleen Stephens home to meet her two older brothers. All that Kathleen knows about her biological parents is that they were of northern European ancestry and Catholic and that the three siblings were born in Portland, Oregon. That's all she wants to know. Her parents are Ray and June Brown. They are the most wonderful parents a girl (or son-in-law, for that matter), could have.

Kathleen's oldest brother, Rocky, is an active genealogist, doing research on the Brown family lines. Kathleen's mother was a member of the LDS Church when the children were born; but her father was not. He joined the Church when the children were still very young. A year later, the family went to the Idaho Falls Temple and was sealed for time and all eternity. Kathleen knows no more about the Catholic Church than most Latter-day Saints. She is devout in her LDS faith and has grown up with a strong LDS heritage. She believes that she was meant from the premortal existence to be with her brothers and her adoptive parents. Because Ray and June Brown were not able to have children, another means was opened for the children to be born and come to live with them. Her physical attributes, keen mind, and natural graces are her genetic heritage from unknown biological parents. Her training and upbringing are the heritage from her adopted parents. Trent sees a number of mannerisms in her facial expressions and behaviors that remind him of her brothers. Her ability to maintain a beautiful, cozy, comfortable home and to raise her children with a strong sense of security and faith, comes from her upbringing. Her natural grace and her ability to make and keep friends, which can lead to long telephone conversations, even with a stranger who has dialed the wrong number, probably comes from a combination of her genetic background and her upbringing.

In this case, memes are stronger than genes. She and Trent met on the front row of a Doctrine and Covenants class at BYU. He was instantly attracted to her physical attributes, resulting from her genes, but what brought them together at BYU was their memes. The many things that she most earnestly wishes to pass on to the next generation come largely from a non-biological heritage. They are her enduring faith in her Savior Jesus Christ and her belief in the restored gospel. The gospel is the strongest of all memes in our lives.

In 2002, Apostle Boyd K. Packer spoke about the lineage function of patriarchal blessings: "In giving a blessing the patriarch may declare our lineage—that is, that we are of Israel, therefore of the family of Abraham, and of a specific tribe of Jacob. In the great majority of cases, Latter-day Saints are of the tribe of Ephraim, the tribe to which has been committed the leadership of the latter-day work. Whether this lineage is of blood or adoption does not matter. This is very important, for it is through the lineage of Abraham alone that the mighty blessings of the Lord for His children on earth are to be accomplished."[3]

Do Latter-day Saints whose patriarchal blessings state that they are of the tribe of Ephraim have any Israelite genetic markers? Would we expect them to? How would one identify such a marker without a standard of comparison? The tribe of Ephraim, as a discrete population, marched off the stage of history over two thousand years ago. There is no recognized population that would represent the gene pool of Ephraim from the time of the Assyrian conquest. Each of us certainly has numerous "bloodlines"—but the expression itself is antiquated and inaccurate. In reality, each of us possesses a mere fraction of the genetic diversity to be found among the thirty ancestors listed on a four-generation pedigree chart. But the realization of the promises to Abraham and Israel have less to do with genetics and more to do with the transmission from one generation to the next of spiritual blessings and opportunities that transcend bloodlines.

Language is another example of the principle of memes. As already discussed, correlation between the ordering of populations on the basis of language and ordering based on genetic groups is often poor. Nephi states that he was educated in the learning of the Jews, and in the language of the Egyptians (1 Ne. 1:2). Later we learn that the Book of Mormon records were kept in "reformed Egyptian." This written language had been handed down through the generations and altered according to their "manner of speech" (Morm. 9:32). It seems that only men of learning could read the records. The language of common usage was Hebrew, but the Nephites had altered it as well. One way a language can be altered in a relatively short period of time is through extended contact and interaction with speakers of another language or languages and the incorporation of native words. This is especially true when the speakers of the original language find themselves in a foreign setting at a loss for words to describe unfamiliar objects and places.

Of course, the influence works in both directions, and the native languages would be expected to quickly incorporate foreign words as well. The British Isles have a striking parallel. The conquerors in 1066 who set themselves up as overlords were Normans—Vikings from France who spoke an altered form of French. The commoners, the Britons, spoke the native Old English. The language of the commoners became altered by interactions with the French-speaking Normans. The language of the priests and the sacred records, the Bible, was Latin, accessible only to the learned. In the end it was the language of the common populace that won out—English. But in the process, the Old English of 1,200 years ago lost 85 percent of its vocabulary, leaving only 15 percent of the original Old English intact a thousand years later.[4] We argue that, in the case of the Nephites in the Americas, it was also the language of the common populace that survived, although considerably altered, while the language of the elite and the sacred language of the scriptures became extinct.

Evidence of contact, influence, or cultural legacy need not rely solely on genetic mechanism of replication and transmission from one generation to the next, or from one populace to another. Memes are an example of an alternate nongenetic form of transmission. The Lehite legacy is unlikely to have left an obvious genetic trace but the memetic legacy is preserved in the message of the Book of Mormon. That message is of Jesus Christ and His covenant with the house of Israel.

Notes

[1]Richard Dawkins, *The Selfish Gene* (Oxford, Eng.: Oxford University Press, 1976), 191-92.

[2]Susan Blackmore, *The Meme Machine* (Oxford, Eng.: Oxford University Press, 1999), ix, 4.

[3]Boyd K. Packer, "The Stake Patriarch," October 5, 2002, *Conference Report* (Salt Lake City: Church of Jesus Christ of Latter-day Saints, 2002), http://www.lds.org/conference/talk/display/0,5232,23-1-315-14,00.html (accessed November 1, 2007).

[4]Albert C. Baugh and Thomas Cable, *A History of the English Language*, 2d ed. (New York: Alfred A. Knopf, 1967), 55.

Chapter Thirteen
Divine Kinship: "No More Strangers or Foreigners"

The concept of a memic ethnic connection rather than a strictly genetic connection is familiar to modern Native Americans. There is a belief among at least some of them that "Indianness should be measured by what's in the heart, not by what's in the blood."[1] There is an increasing trend among such groups toward defining ethnicity as a strictly social—not biological—construct. Eric Beckenhauer noted: "As modern genomic research becomes more commonplace ... the public may become increasingly inclined to subscribe to a theory of genetic essentialism—basically, the notion that our genes determine who we are." However, "there is more genetic variation within a single race than there is among different races. This revelation has had critical implications for the meaning of race, which is now largely considered a social construct, rather than a biological reality."[2]

The concept of social ethnicity existed in ancient Israel. The principle of a social covenant was familiar—in fact, central—to the clannish ancient Israelites. The types and symbolisms are less apparent to us in today's society, except, perhaps, in a nationalistic sense, as in one's patriotic feelings toward a homeland. The covenant originated, says Old Testament scholar Frank Moore Cross not only to regulate kin relationships, but also as a legal means by which the duties and privileges of kinship were extended to another individual or group.[3] Through a covenant with God, ancient Israel became the "kindred of Yahweh." Israel was converted or adopted into the family of God, with each party taking on mutual obligations.

122

The principle of kinship through covenant was acknowledged in the Book of Mormon account as well. The prophet Alma in recounting his vision of Christ said, "Marvel not that all mankind, yea, men and women, all nations, kindreds, tongues and people, must be born again; yea, born of God . . . being redeemed of God, becoming his sons and his daughters" (Mosiah 27:25).

Cross explored the relationship between the concepts of covenant and kinship further: "The social organization of the West Semitic tribal groups was grounded in kinship. Kinship relations defined the rights and obligations, the duties, status and privileges of tribal members. . . . Kinship was conceived in terms of one blood flowing through the veins of the kinship group. Kindred were of one flesh, one bone."[4]

This concept applied not only to the literal family relations, but also to outsiders incorporated into the kin group. The covenant, accompanied by an oath, was a way in which those without genealogical ties could be included within the extended family relations. Israelite marriage was also understood in this context—that the bride entered into a kinship relationship with the groom's tribe. Even the first union, between Adam and Eve, is described in kinship terms. Adam said, "This I know now is bone of my bones, and flesh of my flesh. . . . Therefore shall a man leave his father and his mother and shall cleave unto his wife; and they shall be one flesh" (Moses 3:23–24). The expression, "becoming one flesh" is not referring to the consummation of the couple's union but instead establishes the wife as kin of the first rank. Kindred were of one flesh, of one blood.

Similarly those who take an oath of allegiance to the kin group can be afforded kinship. "Behold I say unto you, that whosoever has heard the words of the prophets, yea, all the holy prophets who have prophesied concerning the coming of the Lord—I say unto you, that all those who have harkened unto their words, and believed that the Lord would redeem his people, and have looked forward to that day for a remission of their sins, I say unto you, that these are his seed, or they are the heirs of the kingdom of God" (Mosiah 15:11).

This passage also highlights one of the duties of a kinsman, i.e., that of redeeming a kinsman sold into debt or slavery. The

Apostle Paul informs us that we are bought with a price, that is, redeemed from the slavery of sin (1 Cor. 6:20). Cross states that, in the tribal religion of the Hebrews, God is the divine Kinsman:

> In the religious sphere, the intimate relationship with the family god, the "God of the Fathers," was expressed in the only language available to members of a tribal society. Their God was the divine Kinsman. . . . [He] fulfills the mutual obligations and receives the privileges of kinship. He leads in battle, redeems from slavery, loves his family, shares the land of his heritage, provides and protects. He blesses those who bless his kindred, curses those who curse his kindred. The family of Yahweh rallies to his call to war, keeps his cultus, obeys his patriarchal commands, maintains familial loyalty, loves him with all their soul[s], and calls on his name.[5]

One mission of Abraham's descendants through Israel was to bear witness of the true and living God unto the nations of the world, and to bring the blessings of his kinship and his covenants to all. Biblical scholar Alfred Edersheim compares this destiny of the Israelites to the New Testament allegory of the mustard seed.[6] The humblest of seeds was destined to grow into the tree in whose branches all the birds of the air would find lodging. In Abraham the stem was pruned down to a single root that sprang up into the *patriarchal* family, then expanded into the *tribes* of Israel, and finally blossomed and bore fruit in the chosen *people*.

The practice and interpretation of the destiny of Israel has differed between Jews and Christians. There is little similarity in the concept of the mission of the covenant. Those among the Jews who still feel there is a mission for Judaism to accomplish do not think in terms of converting the world to Judaism, as many Christians think of converting all to Christianity. The mission is conceived by the orthodox Jew more in terms of living in such a way that others may see that the laws and the ways of those who worship the one God are good, and that He is good.[7] In the extreme interpretation of this form of particularism, all non-Jews have forfeited the opportunity to be counted among the elect of God. Rabbi Benjamin Blech describes this view, "They exist merely to be tolerated or perhaps in

light of how they might serve in God's grander scheme for His chosen people. They are simply vestigial remnants of ancient times and
of peoples who once might have been God's, but are consigned to
the oblivion of divine unconcern."[8]

In contrast, Edersheim describes the embodiment of this heritage, as viewed by the Christian:

> Israel had possessed so to speak, the three crowns of the
> covenant separately. It had the priesthood in Aaron, the royal dignity
> in David and his line, and the prophetic office. But in the last days the
> triple crown of priest, king, and prophet has been united upon Him
> whose crown it really is, even Jesus, a "Prophet like unto Moses," the
> eternal Priest "after the order of Melchizedek," and the real and ever
> reigning "Son of David." And in Him all the promises of God which
> have been given with increasing clearness from Adam onwards to
> Shem, then to Abraham, and to Jacob, in the Law, in the types of the
> Old Testament, and finally in its prophecies, have become "Yea and
> amen," till at the last all nations shall dwell in the tents of Shem.[9]

The Apostle Paul in the New Testament, assured Gentile con-
verts to the new church: "Now therefore ye are no more strangers
and foreigners, but fellow citizens with the saints, and of the household of God" (Eph. 2:19). In his letter to the Gentile Christians of
Galatia, Paul made it plain that all people who have faith in Christ
Jesus and are baptized to his name become the adopted seed of
Abraham, heirs to the mission and joint heirs to the promise inherent in the Abrahamic covenant with God. It is the acceptance and
commitment to the binding terms of the covenant that justify the
recognition of kinship. And yet, what is on the surface a legalistic
arrangement of kinship is considered by the kinsmen as a blood
kinship and treated accordingly.

The Lord declared to Abraham:

> And I will make of thee a great nation, and I will bless thee
> above measure, and make thy name great among all nations, and
> thou shalt be a blessing unto thy seed after thee, that in their hands
> they shall bear this ministry and Priesthood unto all nations;

And I will bless them through thy name; for as many as receive this Gospel shall be called after thy name, and shall be accounted thy seed, and shall rise up and bless thee, as their father. (Abr. 2:9–10)

But where is the archeological or genetic evidence of Abraham? "Was there ever, thousands of years ago, a personage named Abraham," asked *National Geographic* writer Tad Szulc, "whom more than three billion people—more than half of humanity—venerate as the father, patriarch, and spiritual ancestor of their faiths (2 billion Christians, 1.5 billion Muslims, 15 million Jews)?"[10] Neither in Babylon nor Egypt is an archeological trace of Abraham to be found. Manfred Bietak, chairman of the Institute of Egyptology at the University of Vienna, said, "Absolutely blank. As far as the Egyptians are concerned, it's as if Abraham never set foot in the delta."[11] The study of the DNA of male Jews and Middle Eastern Arabs—among them Syrians, Palestinians, and Lebanese—shows that they share a common set of ancestors, but none can be specifically identified as Abraham. Continues Szulc, "Today he stands as a unique spiritual figure, transcending the frontiers of great religions. However questionable the accuracy of the scriptures, however thin the archeological and historical evidence, Jews, Christians, and Muslims still revere him as the patriarch."[12] The Abrahamic covenant is an example of a meme. That meme—Abraham's testimony of one God—changed the world forever.

Ultimately, in a modern era of mobility and diversity, the matter comes down to a personal commitment to values and beliefs, and participation in the fellowship of believers while living in a broader community. It has less to do with genealogy or bloodlines or tribal affiliations. The Abrahamic covenant, reestablished as the new and everlasting covenant of the gospel of Jesus Christ, is extended to all. Those who embrace it become God's "people."

These concepts of kinship bear directly on the Book of Mormon account of a "branch of Israel grown over the wall" (Gen. 49:22). From a small colony under the leadership of Nephi a kinship was established within the grouping of a larger resident population. In effect, it was perceived as a situation of "them and us"—Lamanites and Nephites. This perception differs little from the concept of "Jew and Gentile." "Gentile" encompasses all non-Jews. With the final destruction of the Nephite kinship, all who remained on the Americas were in effect "Lamanites." If this interpretation is correct, then the recently revised introduction to the Book of Mormon is completely accurate: "After thousands of years, all were destroyed except the Lamanites, and they are among the ancestors of the American Indians." All Native Americans are, in fact, descended from these people who appear as "Lamanites" and "Gentiles" in the record of Nephi's people. Lehi's prophecy to Laman and Lemuel was realized. Their memetic heritage of dissension continued, even if their genetic markers may not have. The revised wording of the Introduction appears to acknowledge the non-exclusive and perhaps minor contribution to the modern Native American gene pool by the "Lamanites"—at least those specific to the Nephites' immediate sphere of interaction.

Having said that, we cannot conclude this book without a final comment about the evidence that continues to accumulate relevant to the historicity of this unique book of scripture. There is growing evidence for trans-oceanic contacts between the Old World and the New World that challenges the paradigm of an isolated Western Hemisphere singularly colonized by a founder population from Siberia. The more we learn of history and archeology, the clearer it becomes that the entire world has always been a melting pot of populations. "This evidence cannot be ignored by any serious person who hopes to call himself a scholar, of whatever religious persuasion," concluded two evangelical scholars who, when they began to examine Mormon scholarship, were surprised at the numbers of Mormon scholars, at their training, their sophistication, and their intellectual conclusions regarding the historicity of the Book of Mormon.[13]

As God promised Abraham, remnants of the house of Israel have been scattered among all nations of the earth, like leaven in bread. We all benefit from our genetic and memetic heritage from the house of Israel but we probably will never find genetic traces of the leaven in most nations. We probably will never find a genetic marker for the children of Lehi, for the children of Israel, or for the children of God. Ultimately, we have concluded that the fundamental question of the veracity of Book of Mormon claims lie beyond the ken of modern DNA research. The necessary experiment is a very personal one. The final implications of the book, as a witness of the prophetic calling of Joseph Smith and as another testament of the divinity of Jesus Christ, remain squarely, and perhaps appropriately, within the realm of faith and individual testimony.

Notes

[1] Eric Beckenhauer, "Redefining Race: Can Genetic Testing Provide Biological Proof of Indian Ethnicity?" *Stanford Law Review* 56 (2003): 161–90.

[2] Ibid., 175.

[3] Frank Moore Cross, quoted in Hershel Shanks, "God as Divine Kinsman: What Covenant Meant in Ancient Israel," *Biblical Archeology Review*, July/August 1999, 32–33, 60–66; see also Frank Moore Cross, *From Epic to Canon: History and Literature in Ancient Israel* (Baltimore, Md.: Johns Hopkins University Press, 1998).

[4] Cross, quoted in Shanks, "God as Divine Kinsman," 32.

[5] Cross, quoted in ibid., 33.

[6] Alfred Edersheim, *Bible History: Old Testament* (Grand Rapids, Mich.: William B. Eerdmans Publishing, 1982).

[7] Ellis T. Rasmussen, "Judaism," *Ensign*, March 1971, 49.

[8] Benjamin Blech, *Understanding Judaism: The Basics of Deed and Creed* (Northvale, N.J.: Jason Aronson, 1991).

[9] Edersheim, *Bible History*.

[10] Tad Szulc, "Abraham," *National Geographic*, December 2001, 96.

[11] Manfred Bietak, quoted in ibid., 118.

[12] Ibid., 129.

[13] Carl Mosser and Paul Owens, "Mormon Scholarship, Apologetics, and Evangelical Neglect: Losing the Battle and Not Knowing It?" *Trinity Journal* 19 (1998): 179–205.

Index

A

abandoned villages and cities in Mesoamerica, 101

Abraham. *See also* covenant.
  covenant of
    also applied to Western Hemisphere, 7, 8 note 7, 9–13
    to bless all nations, 125–26
    no archaeological or genetic evidence of, 126

absence of evidence. *See* negative, proving.

Adam and Eve, union of as establishing kinship, 123

adenine (A), 36

admixture
  and allele frequencies, 42
  and Human Genome Diversity Project, 50–51
  as challenge to DNA conclusions, 7
  impact of on modern populations, 28, 42
  in Colombia, 66

in South American haplogroups, 66
  of Europeans and Africans with Native Americans, 50, 54–55

adoption. *See also* covenant.
  extends kinship relations to outsiders, 123–27
  of believers into house of Israel, 10, 119
  of Kathleen Brown Stephens, 118–19

Afrikaners, influence of founder effect on, 42

albinism, as example of allele defect, 33–35, 38

allegory of the olive tree, 93–94

alleles
  and individual variations, 41
  and population characteristics, 42
  determine heterozygosity/ homozygosity, 33
  frequency of and population size, 44
  functioning of, 33–40
  61.4 million by tenth generation, 86

D. Jeffrey Meldrum, Ph.D. is an associate professor of anatomy and anthropology at Idaho State University since 1994 and an affiliate curator of vertebrate paleontology at the Idaho Museum of Natural History. With degrees from Brigham Young University and the State University of New York at Stony Brook, he has post-doctoral and lecturing experience at Duke University, the Northwestern University Medical School, and the Chicago Center for Religion and Science. At ISU, he teaches human anatomy, organic evolution, and primate studies with a research focus on human bipedalism and field work in Argentina, Colombia, and the Intermountain West. Jeff's callings have included a mission (Germany), Gospel Doctrine and Primary teacher, elders' quorum president, bishop's counselor, and, currently, family history consultant. The father of six sons, he recently completed seven years as Scoutmaster.

Trent D. Stephens, Ph.D., is a professor of anatomy and embryology at Idaho State University. With degrees from Brigham Young University and the University of Pennsylvania, he previously taught anatomy at the University of Washington's Medical School and has been teaching anatomy and embryology at Idaho State University since 1981. An award-winning teacher and researcher, Trent investigates the developmental origins of vertebrate form and has published more than eighty scientific papers and books, including several leading textbooks for anatomy and physiology. After his mission (Great Lakes), his callings have included elders' quorum president, stake high council, bishop twice and, currently, high priest group leader. Long a Scouter, he is a Woodbadge graduate and was awarded the Silver Beaver (1991). Trent and Kathleen have five children and ten grandchildren.

Also available from
GREG KOFFORD BOOKS

The Brigham Young University Book of Mormon Symposium Series

Various Authors

Nine-volume paperback box set, ISBN: 978-1-58958-087-9

A series of lectures delivered at BYU by a wide and exciting array of the finest gospel scholars in the Church. Get valuable insights from foremost authorities including General authorities, BYU Professors and Church Educational System instructors. No gospel library will be complete without this valuable resource. Anyone interested in knowing what the top gospel scholars in the Church are saying about such important subjects as historiography, geography, and faith in Christ will be sure to enjoy this handsome box set. This is the perfect gift for any student of the Book of Mormon.

Contributors include: Neal A. Maxwell, Boyd K. Packer, Jeffrey R. Holland, Russell M. Nelson, Dallin H. Oaks, Gerald N. Lund, Dean L. Larsen, Joseph Fielding McConkie, Richard Neitzel Holzapfel, Truman G. Madsen, John W. Welch, Robert J. Matthews, Daniel H. Ludlow, Stephen D. Ricks, Grant Underwood, Robert L. Millet, Susan Easton Black, H. Donl Peterson, John L. Sorenson, Monte S. Nyman, Daniel C. Peterson, Stephen E. Robinson, Carolyn J. Rasmus, Dennis L. Largey, C. Max Caldwell, Andrew C. Skinner, S. Michael Wilcox, Paul R. Cheesman, K. Douglas Bassett, Douglas E. Brinley, Richard O. Cowan, Donald W. Parry, Bruce A. Van Orden, Kenneth W. Anderson, Leland Gentry, S. Kent Brown, H. Dean Garrett, Lee L. Donaldson, Robert E. Parsons, S. Brent Farley, Rodney Turner, Larry E. Dahl, Mae Blanch, Rex C. Reeve Jr., E. Dale LeBaron, Clyde J. Williams, Chauncey C. Riddle, Kent P. Jackson, Daniel K. Judd, Neal E. Lambert, Michael W. Middleton, R. Wayne Shute, John M. Butler, and many more!

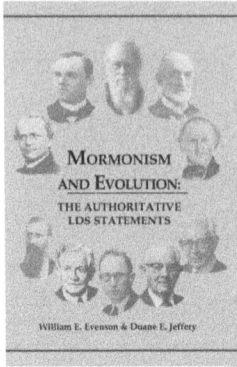

Mormonism and Evolution: The Authoritative LDS Statements

Edited by William E. Evenson and Duane E. Jeffrey

Paperback, ISBN: 978-1-58958-093-0

The Church of Jesus Christ of Latter-day Saints (the Mormon Church) has generally been viewed by the public as anti-evolutionary in its doctrine and teachings. But official statements on the subject by the Church's highest governing quorum and/or president have been considerably more open and diverse than is popularly believed.

This book compiles in full all known authoritative statements (either authored or formally approved for publication) by the Church's highest leaders on the topics of evolution and the origin of human beings. The editors provide historical context for these statements that allows the reader to see what stimulated the issuing of each particular document and how they stand in relation to one another.

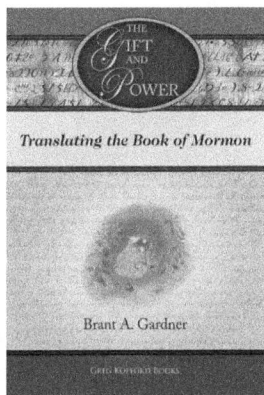

The Gift and Power: Translating the Book of Mormon

Brant A. Gardner

Hardcover, ISBN: 978-1-58958-131-9

From Brant A. Gardner, the author of the highly praised *Second Witness* commentaries on the Book of Mormon, comes *The Gift and Power: Translating the Book of Mormon*. In this first book-length treatment of the translation process, Gardner closely examines the accounts surrounding Joseph Smith's translation of the Book of Mormon to answer a wide spectrum of questions about the process, including: Did the Prophet use seerstones common to folk magicians of his time? How did he use them? And, what is the relationship to the golden plates and the printed text?

Approaching the topic in three sections, part 1 examines the stories told about Joseph, folk magic, and the translation. Part 2 examines the available evidence to determine how closely the English text replicates the original plate text. And part 3 seeks to explain how seer stones worked, why they no longer work, and how Joseph Smith could have produced a translation with them.

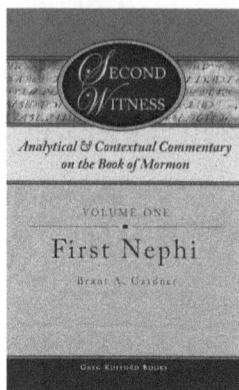

Second Witness:
Analytical and Contextual Commentatry on the Book of Mormon

Brant A. Gardner

Second Witness, a new six-volume series from Greg Kofford Books, takes a detailed, verse-by-verse look at the Book of Mormon. It marshals the best of modern scholarship and new insights into a consistent picture of the Book of Mormon as a historical document. Taking a faithful but scholarly approach to the text and reading it through the insights of linguistics, anthropology, and ethnohistory, the commentary approaches the text from a variety of perspectives: how it was created, how it relates to history and culture, and what religious insights it provides.

The commentary accepts the best modern scholarship, which focuses on a particular region of Mesoamerica as the most plausible location for the Book of Mormon's setting. For the first time, that location—its peoples, cultures, and historical trends—are used as the backdrop for reading the text. The historical background is not presented as proof, but rather as an explanatory context.

The commentary does not forget Mormon's purpose in writing. It discusses the doctrinal and theological aspects of the text and highlights the way in which Mormon created it to meet his goal of "convincing . . . the Jew and Gentile that Jesus is the Christ, the Eternal God."

Praise for the *Second Witness* series:

"Gardner not only provides a unique tool for understanding the Book of Mormon as an ancient document written by real, living prophets, but he sets a standard for Latter-day Saint thinking and writing about scripture, providing a model for all who follow. . . . No other reference source will prove as thorough and valuable for serious readers of the Book of Mormon."

-Neal A. Maxwell Institute, Brigham Young University

1. 1st Nephi: 978-1-58958-041-1

2. 2nd Nephi–Jacob: 978-1-58958-042-8

3. Enos–Mosiah: 978-1-58958-043-5

4. Alma: 978-1-58958-044-2

5. Helaman–3rd Nephi: 978-1-58958-045-9

6. 4th Nephi–Moroni: 978-1-58958-046-6

Complete set: 978-1-58958-047-3

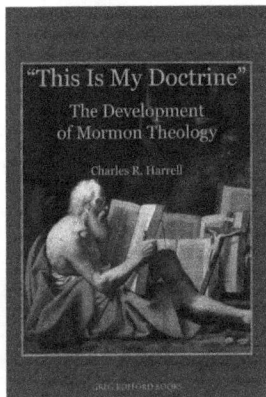

"This is My Doctrine":
The Development of Mormon Theology

Charles R. Harrell

Hardcover, ISBN: 978-1-58958-103-6

The principal doctrines defining Mormonism today often bear little resemblance to those it started out with in the early 1830s. This book shows that these doctrines did not originate in a vacuum but were rather prompted and informed by the religious culture from which Mormonism arose. Early Mormons, like their early Christian and even earlier Israelite predecessors, brought with them their own varied culturally conditioned theological presuppositions (a process of convergence) and only later acquired a more distinctive theological outlook (a process of differentiation).

In this first-of-its-kind comprehensive treatment of the development of Mormon theology, Charles Harrell traces the history of Latter-day Saint doctrines from the times of the Old Testament to the present. He describes how Mormonism has carried on the tradition of the biblical authors, early Christians, and later Protestants in reinterpreting scripture to accommodate new theological ideas while attempting to uphold the integrity and authority of the scriptures. In the process, he probes three questions: How did Mormon doctrines develop? What are the scriptural underpinnings of these doctrines? And what do critical scholars make of these same scriptures? In this enlightening study, Harrell systematically peels back the doctrinal accretions of time to provide a fresh new look at Mormon theology.

"This Is My Doctrine" will provide those already versed in Mormonism's theological tradition with a new and richer perspective of Mormon theology. Those unacquainted with Mormonism will gain an appreciation for how Mormon theology fits into the larger Jewish and Christian theological traditions.

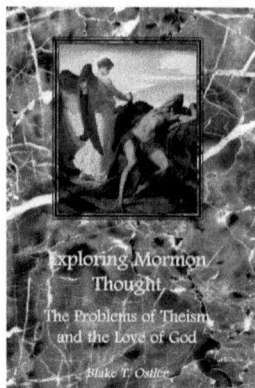

Exploring Mormon Thought Series

Blake T. Ostler

IN VOLUME ONE, *The Attributes of God*, Blake T. Ostler explores Christian and Mormon notions about God. ISBN: 978-1-58958-003-9

IN VOLUME TWO, *The Problems of Theism and the Love of God*, Blake Ostler explores issues related to soteriology, or the theory of salvation. ISBN: 978-1-58958-095-4

IN VOLUME THREE, *Of God and Gods*, Ostler analyzes and responds to the arguments of contemporary international theologians, reconstructs and interprets Joseph Smith's important King Follett Discourse and Sermon in the Grove, and argues persuasively for the Mormon doctrine of "robust deification." ISBN: 978-1-58958-107-4

Praise for the *Exploring Mormon Thought* series:

"These books are the most important works on Mormon theology ever written. There is nothing currently available that is even close to the rigor and sophistication of these volumes. B. H. Roberts and John A. Widtsoe may have had interesting insights in the early part of the twentieth century, but they had neither the temperament nor the training to give a rigorous defense of their views in dialogue with a wider stream of Christian theology. Sterling McMurrin and Truman Madsen had the capacity to engage Mormon theology at this level, but neither one did."

—Neal A. Maxwell Institute, Brigham Young University

Hugh Nibley:
A Consecrated Life

Boyd Jay Petersen

Hardcover, ISBN: 978-1-58958-019-0

Winner of the Mormon History Association's Best Biography Award

As one of the LDS Church's most widely recognized scholars, Hugh Nibley is both an icon and an enigma. Through complete access to Nibley's correspondence, journals, notes, and papers, Petersen has painted a portrait that reveals the man behind the legend.

Starting with a foreword written by Zina Nibley Petersen and finishing with appendices that include some of the best of Nibley's personal correspondence, the biography reveals aspects of the tapestry of the life of one who has truly consecrated his life to the service of the Lord.

Praise for *A Consecrated Life*:

"Hugh Nibley is generally touted as one of Mormonism's greatest minds and perhaps its most prolific scholarly apologist. Just as hefty as some of Nibley's largest tomes, this authorized biography is delightfully accessible and full of the scholar's delicious wordplay and wit, not to mention some astonishing war stories and insights into Nibley's phenomenal acquisition of languages. Introduced by a personable foreword from the author's wife (who is Nibley's daughter), the book is written with enthusiasm, respect and insight. . . . On the whole, Petersen is a careful scholar who provides helpful historical context. . . . This project is far from hagiography. It fills an important gap in LDS history and will appeal to a wide Mormon audience."
—Publishers Weekly

"Well written and thoroughly researched, Petersen's biography is a must-have for anyone struggling to reconcile faith and reason."
—Greg Taggart, Association for Mormon Letters

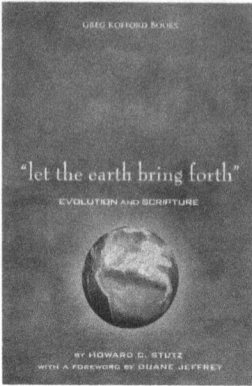

"Let the Earth Bring Forth"
Evolution and Scripture

Howard C. Stutz

Paperback, ISBN: 978-1-58958-126-5

A century ago in 1809, Charles Darwin was born. Fifty years later, he published a scientific treatise describing the process of speciation that launched what appeared to be a challenge to the traditional religious interpretation of how life was created on earth. The controversy has erupted anew in the last decade as Creationists and Young Earth adherents challenge school curricula and try to displace "the theory of evolution."

This book is filled with fascinating examples of speciation by the well-known process of mutation but also by the less well-known processes of sexual recombination and polyploidy. In addition to the fossil record, Howard Stutz examines the evidence from the embryo stages of human beings and other creatures to show how selection and differentiation moved development in certain favored directions while leaving behind evidence of earlier, discarded developments. Anatomy, biochemistry, and genetics are all examined in their turn.

With rigorously scientific clarity but in language accessible to a popular audience, the book proceeds to its conclusion, reached after a lifetime of study: the divine map of creation is one supported by both scientific evidence and the scriptures. This is a book to be read, not only for its fascinating scientific insights, but also for a new appreciation of well-known scriptures.